IN
AMERICAN
HISTORY

WITHDRAWN

ALCATRAZ PRISON IN AMERICAN HISTORY

Marilyn Tower Oliver

E **Enslow Publishers, Inc.**

40 Industrial Road   PO Box 38
Box 398   Aldershot
Berkeley Heights, NJ 07922 Hants GU12 6BP
USA   UK

http://www.enslow.com

Dedication

For my son, Scott, who has always enjoyed American history, and for my daughter, Lauren, and niece, Ann Oliver Graybill, who accompanied me to The Rock.

Library of Congress Cataloging-in-Publication Data

Oliver, Marilyn Tower.
    Alcatraz Prison in American history / Marilyn Tower Oliver.
        p. cm. — (In American history)
    Includes bibliographical references and index.
    Summary: Traces the development of the federal prison at Alcatraz Island from the days of Spanish exploration, through its years as a military prison, to its fame as the most escape-proof prison in America.
    ISBN 0-89490-990-8
        1. United States Penitentiary, Alcatraz Island, California—History—Juvenile literature. 2. Military Prison at Alcatraz Island, California—History—Juvenile literature. 3. Prisons—California—Alcatraz Island—History—Juvenile literature. 4. Alcatraz Island (Calif.)—History—Juvenile literature. [1. Alcatraz Island (Calif.)—History. 2. Prisons—History.] I. Title. II. Series.
    HV9474.A4055 1998
    365'.979461—dc21   97-32453
                                           CIP
                                           AC

Printed in the United States of America

10 9 8 7 6 5 4 3 2

Illustration Credits: Courtesy, Golden Gate National Parks Association, p. 67; Courtesy, Golden Gate NRA, pp. 54, 61, 70, 100, 102, 114; Workman and Temple Family Homestead Museum, City of Industry, California, pp. 19, 20; Marilyn T. Oliver, pp. 10, 13, 31, 63, 65, 116, 118; National Archives, pp. 24, 26, 29, 34, 40, 52, 80, 83; Photo Courtesy of *The Oakland Tribune*, p. 112; Reproduced with the permission of the estate of Harold M. Bacon, p. 90.

Cover Illustration: Courtesy, Golden Gate NRA; Marilyn T. Oliver; National Archives.

★ CONTENTS ★

★ ACKNOWLEDGMENTS ★

Special thanks to Paul R. Spitzzeri of the Homestead Museum, City of Industry; to the Golden Gate National Park Association; and to Irene A. Stachura of the J. Porter Shaw Library, San Francisco National Maritime Historic Park.

THE ROCK

At eight in the evening on August 18, 1934, without warning, some of the most dangerous inmates at the federal prison in Atlanta were ordered from their cells to be stripped, searched, and given new clothing. The men were told they were going to be moved and that they could take no personal belongings, not even family pictures.

The prisoners were handcuffed and were leg ironed together, two by two, and marched to the prison yard, where a train waited. They boarded the two passenger cars, which were built with special safety features to ensure that the men inside could not escape. Steel bars fitted with closely meshed wire screens blocked the windows of the cars. In each car, two guards were posted. They were unarmed to avoid the possibility that a prisoner could seize their weapons and stage an escape. At both ends of the cars, protected from the inmates by wire-screened cages, armed guards carried shotguns. At 5:00 A.M. on August 19, Atlanta prison warden

Arthur Alderhold boarded, and the train pulled away. For the inmates onboard, the destination was unknown. Only the train's crew and the officials onboard knew the route the train would take.

During the cross-country trip, special security precautions were observed. At every stop along the way, armed guards stood on the train platforms. The baggage car was outfitted with additional weapons and a guard. The high level of security was considered necessary because authorities feared an escape attempt might occur in this transfer. Many of the prisoners on the train had escape records.

Three and a half days later, at 8:20 P.M. on August 22, the heavily fortified train pulled into Tiburon, a town on San Francisco Bay. Secrecy surrounded the arrival. When the train pulled into Tiburon, it was met by a large, flat-bottomed boat called a barge. The coaches holding the prisoners were backed onto the barge as a Coast Guard commander watched from a nearby boat. Although authorities had tried to keep the trip a secret, news had leaked out. Three hundred yards away from the barge, reporters in boats tried to get a glimpse of the men inside the train cars.[1]

The excitement and interest that surrounded this event was caused by the opening of a new, federal prison on Alcatraz, an island in San Francisco Bay. America had never had such a prison before. It would be considered the most secure prison in the world. In magazine and newspaper stories, reporters called Alcatraz "America's Devil's Island" after a French high-security prison on the coast of South America. Alcatraz prison was known as The Rock because it was on a twelve-acre rocky, sandstone island. The security devices at the prison were the most advanced of their time. The steel bars on many of the windows and cells could not be cut with files. Locks could only be opened mechanically by two guards located in different positions. Electronic metal detectors could reveal hidden pistols or knives on prisoners and visitors. Barbed wire surrounded the compound of concrete cells. Most important, a mile and a half of water separated the prison from the city of San Francisco on the mainland. Dangerous currents that could sweep a swimmer out into the Pacific Ocean made the distance almost impossible to swim. The water was often very cold. Boats from the prison and the Coast Guard patrolled the waters around the island.[2]

Alcatraz Federal Penitentiary was designed to house prisoners who had been troublemakers in other federal prisons. The men who were imprisoned at Alcatraz lived a life run by strict rules and routine. Women prisoners were not sent there.

The new arrivals joined thirty-two prisoners left behind when the military prison run by the United

A prisoner's first view of Alcatraz would be of the guards' barracks and of the dock.

States Army on Alcatraz Island closed. These military convicts were among the most difficult prisoners held by the army. They had been convicted of serious crimes such as murder, rape, robbery, and assault.[3]

After the fifty-three convicts were unloaded at the island dock, they hiked slowly up the steep hill. Some of them were barefoot because their feet were too swollen from the leg irons to wear the loose slippers they had been issued.

Warden James A. Johnston wrote that the prisoners were "hot, dirty, weary, unshaved, depressed, desperate, showing plainly that they felt they were at the end of the trail."[4]

In September 1934, a second shipment of prisoners to Alcatraz brought 103 more inmates. By the end of 1934, there were 211 inmates at the prison.

During the time Alcatraz was a federal prison, the Bureau of Prisons, the federal agency in charge of prisons, had a policy of secrecy about the treatment of prisoners. Visitors were discouraged. Boats that sailed too close to the island were warned to keep three hundred yards from shore. Those that did not ran the risk of being fired upon. Rarely were members of the press allowed to visit the island.

Stories about the inhumane treatment of prisoners came from inmates who were released or paroled. When William Henry Ambrose was paroled in July 1935, he told reporters about the torment of being a prisoner. He said that the strict rule of silence, in which inmates were not allowed to speak to each other, was a form of psychological torture. In an interview with the *San Francisco Chronicle* he said that the no-talk rule was the hardest thing for prisoners. He said, "Not a word can be spoken by any of the convicts in line, at the table, at work, or in their cells. . . . It's the toughest pen I've ever seen. The hopelessness of it gets to you."[5]

When inmate Roy Gardner was released in 1938, he wrote a book titled *Hellcatraz: The Rock of Despair.* He said that the inmates in the prison gave up hope because of the strict rules and the monotony of day-to-day life.[6] The prison's location also added to the feeling of despair. Prisoners could look through the barred windows at the tall buildings and intense beauty of San Francisco just a few miles away. Freedom seemed close at hand, but escape was almost impossible because of the dangerous currents, icy waters, and high security.

Nevertheless, there were many escape attempts during the twenty-nine years that Alcatraz served as a federal prison. The most famous attempt occurred on June 11, 1962, when three inmates were able to sneak out of the prison through tunnels they had dug in the concrete walls. They crawled to the roof, climbed the fence, and disappeared. They were never heard from again, and their bodies were never found. The escape attempt remains one of the mysteries of Alcatraz.

Although many of America's toughest criminals were housed at Alcatraz, no one was ever executed there. Inmates condemned to death were sent to San Quentin, a state penitentiary north of San Francisco. Prisoners did die at Alcatraz, however. Eight prisoners were murdered by other inmates. There were five suicides, and fifteen inmates died from illness.[7]

Inmates looked through the barred windows at the beautiful view of San Francisco—so near and yet so far away.

The harsh prison life at Alcatraz has been portrayed in many movies, adding to the legend that continues to fascinate us even years after the prison has been closed. Now part of the Golden Gate National Recreation Area, Alcatraz Island attracts many visitors from all over the world each year. The visitors have an avid fascination in exploring the now empty prison where America's most wanted men once lived. As visitors walk past the vacant cells, they may wonder about the prisoners who were housed here. Some of the cells are open so that a visitor can step inside to actually feel the confining limits of the small, enclosed space. Some may think about how one might make an escape.

Most of these visitors are unaware that Alcatraz Federal Penitentiary is but one chapter in the island's colorful history. For many centuries, the island was inhabited mainly by birds such as the pelicans for which it is named. *Alcatraz* means pelican in Spanish. In the long distant past, the island was visited by American Indians who lived in small groups along the shores of what is now known as San Francisco Bay. It has also been the site of a lighthouse, a fort, and a military prison. Today, it is one of San Francisco's most popular tourist attractions.

Let's take a step back in time to look at the early years of Alcatraz Island and the unique role it has played in American history.

Thousands of years ago, Alcatraz Island was the peak of a sandstone mountain that lay in a valley near the Pacific Ocean. When the ice that covered a large part of the earth's surface began to melt, the level of water in the ocean began to rise. Water rushed through a gap in the mountains along the California coast, flooding much of the valley, creating San Francisco Bay. Only the tip of the mountain remained above water and became the island now known as Alcatraz. The ocean waters separated the island from the mainland around the bay.

EARLY SETTLEMENTS

The first humans in the area were American Indians from the Coastal Miwok and the Costanoan tribes, who settled along the shores of the bay. Although it is believed they came about ten thousand years ago, it is possible that they lived in the area before the floods. Archaeologists have found the remains of several villages on nearby Angel Island, which had springs and streams. It is unlikely that anyone lived on

Alcatraz because it has no freshwater. Some historians believe that early people feared the island was haunted. Others think they braved the dangerous currents to sail there in canoes made of reeds. They came to hunt and gather eggs from the nests of the many birds living on Alcatraz.[1]

Spanish Exploration

Life continued in much the same pattern for many years until 1769. Although Spanish ships had sailed the waters of the Pacific since 1542, they had always missed the narrow opening to San Francisco Bay, which was often obscured by fog. Today, the entrance is called the Golden Gate. In 1542 when the Spanish explorer Juan Rodriguez Cabrillo sailed along the coast of California, he claimed all of Alta (Upper) California for the king of Spain. Many years passed without much further exploration. However, toward the end of the eighteenth century, fur traders from Great Britain and Russia appeared along the western coast of America to hunt the skins of sea otters and seals. The Spanish worried that these traders might claim California for their countries. The Spaniards decided to take action.

In 1769 a land party was sent from Baja (Lower) California to explore the California coast as far north as Monterey Bay. The leader of the group was Captain

Gaspar de Portola. The group was ordered to establish a military fort and civilian settlement at Monterey. Although Monterey Bay was known, no one had visited there for over one hundred years. Unknowingly, the group passed by Monterey Bay without recognizing it and continued north, stopping a few miles south of the Golden Gate. A group was sent to explore the land.

San Francisco Bay was then discovered by accident when one member of the group, Sergeant Jose Ortega, looked out from a hilltop. The Spaniards were astonished by the size of the bay, but had no boats to sail across it. Fearing his men might suffer during the winter cold, Portola returned to San Diego, a Spanish settlement to the south. Ashamed that he had not found Monterey Bay, he wrote that his group had not discovered anything.

The soldiers, however, talked about the huge bay they had found. News reached the military officials, who decided to send more scouting parties.

Three years passed before another Spanish group returned, this time with orders to determine the size of the bay. Captain Pedro Fages stood on the hills to the east of the bay and looked westward. He recorded that there were five islands in the harbor.

A few years later, in 1775, the first recorded ship, the *San Carlos*, sailed into the bay. The commander of the ship, Juan Manuel de Ayala, described the geological features of the bay. Ayala and the ship's pilot set out to chart and name the landmarks in the bay in order to create a map. Ayala described an island that was very barren and rocky. He wrote that "the island was so barren and craggy that it could provide no shelter even for small craft and it was called Alcatraces [Pelicans] because of the large numbers of them that were there." When Ayala made his map, however, he gave the name Alcatraces to the present-day Yerba Buena Island. The present-day Alcatraz Island was unnamed.[2]

In 1827 Captain Frederick Beechey, a British officer, made a second survey of San Francisco Bay. He switched the name Alcatraces to the unnamed rocky island. He also changed the spelling of the "Island of the Pelicans" to "Alcatrasses." This was the first of many misspellings and name changes. Through the American Civil War, the island was called Alcatraces, Alcatrasses, Alcatrazes, Alcatrasas, and other variations of the word. The Americans who came in search of gold called the island "Bird Island" or "White Island."[3]

In 1822 when Mexico gained independence from Spain, California became Mexican territory. Although Alcatraz was now under the control of Mexico, there was little interest in developing the rocky island. On June 8, 1846, Julian Workman, a naturalized Mexican citizen, obtained a land grant for the island. He was ordered by Pío Pico, the Mexican governor of

California, to build a navigation light on the island as soon as possible. Workman ignored the order and gave the title of the island to his son-in-law, Francis Temple. Many changes were taking place at this time. On May 3, 1846, the United States declared war on Mexico. American troops occupied California. On July 7, the American flag was raised in Monterey. The following day, the U.S.S. *Portsmouth* dropped anchor in the bay. On July 9, 1846, Commander John B. Montgomery ordered that the American flag be raised above the plaza as troops on the ship fired a twenty-one gun salute.[4]

In 1846, Julian Workman petitioned Governor Pío Pico to buy Alcatraz Island. He was granted the island on June 8, 1846.

Francis Temple then sold the island to John C. Frémont, the new American governor of California, for five thousand dollars. Temple said that he was never paid. Frémont answered that he had given Temple a bond for the purchase price in his capacity as governor of California. The United States government, however, said Frémont did not have authority to make the purchase. So Frémont paid the five thousand

Soon after he received Alcatraz, Workman gave the island to his son-in-law, Francis Temple (shown here). When California became a territory of the United States, Temple sold Alcatraz to the American governor, John C. Frémont.

dollars from his own funds and said the land belonged to him. The government, however, still claimed Alcatraz as federal property. A lawsuit between Frémont and the government followed, continuing for some time before the United States Army occupied the island.[5]

The army had long been interested in the strategic location of the island. In 1847, less than a year after American troops occupied California, Lieutenant William H. Warner surveyed the island. His report stated that the island had no resources, but it was in a perfect location for fortifications to guard the bay.

Throughout this time, the Mexican-American War continued. In 1848 the United States won. Among the Mexican territories granted to the United States was California. Early in the same year, gold was discovered by James Marshall at a sawmill on the American River in the Sierra Nevada foothills of California. When word spread to the East Coast and to other parts of the world, men rushed to California to try their luck in the goldfields.

California's population began to grow quickly. In 1850 California became a state. By 1860, San Francisco was the twelfth-largest urban center in the United States and the principal port on the West Coast.

Alcatraz Island was about to enter a new phase in its history.

FORT AND
LIGHTHOUSE

The gold rush of 1849 made San Francisco the largest population center and the most important port on the West Coast. Protecting the city and the bay from foreign enemies who might try to attack from the Pacific was a high priority for the United States government. Alcatraz Island was also considered a fine location for a lighthouse and fort.

Army engineers had surveyed and described Alcatraz in 1847. They noted that the rocky island was covered only by a thin crust of earth. Soon they began to haul soil from nearby Angel Island to pile in front of the large guns that they planned to set up on Alcatraz. The dirt would absorb the impact of enemy shells. The soil sprouted some of the plants found on Alcatraz today. Trees and plants were also brought to the island in the 1850s. In the 1860s, pits were cut and dynamited into the rock, and filled with dirt. Many of the animals and insects that live on Alcatraz were probably introduced at that time.[1]

Building on Alcatraz proved to be a difficult task for the army. The only place for ships to land was on the eastern side of the island. The construction of fortifications was assigned to First Lieutenant Zealous Bates Tower. He ordered a wharf built in the cove on the eastern side of the island so that supplies could be brought in. The workers blasted and cut away at the island's slopes. Because the rocky island proved unstable, retaining walls had to be built.

Construction of the fortifications required many workers. By 1857 there were one hundred fifty laborers working on the island. By 1861 it was proposed that 124 large guns be placed on the island. The weapons were to be six-inch-, eight-inch-, and ten-inch-caliber cannons, capable of firing solid iron shot, hollow explosive shells, or heated cannonballs to set fire to wooden warships. Smaller caliber howitzers were to be mounted in the guardhouse for close-in defense.[2]

The next year, construction began on a huge barracks to house the officers and enlisted men stationed on the island. This building, known as the Citadel, was surrounded by a moat and had a drawbridge.

When Tower was transferred, the task of construction was handed over to Lieutenant Frederick Prime in 1857, then to Second Lieutenant James Birdseye McPherson. On December 30, 1859, Company H of the Third Artillery occupied Alcatraz, beginning a seventy-seven-year administration of the island by the United States Army.[3]

The Lighthouse

As more and more ships sailed into San Francisco Bay, the dangers of navigating without lighthouses became apparent. Many ships were sunk or stranded trying to reach the Golden Gate. In 1850 Congress budgeted $120,000 to build lighthouses in California and Oregon. Alcatraz lighthouse was the first to be built

The first lighthouse on Alcatraz Island was commissioned in 1854. The building on the left is the post headquarters.

on the Pacific Coast. The forty-foot-tall lighthouse began service on June 1, 1854. Its light could be seen by ships fourteen miles out to sea.

Often in San Francisco Bay, there were strong winds and dense fogs, which made it hard for ships to stay on course. To help ships navigate through the foggy bay, the lighthouse had a fog bell that weighed a thousand pounds. It took one man forty-five minutes to wind up the bell. After it was wound, the bell would ring six times a minute, once every ten seconds. The sounds would last for five hours. Then the bell would have to be rewound. A larger bell was installed in 1881.[4]

In 1909, when the army built a prison cell house, the new building blocked the light from the lighthouse. The army decided to tear down the old lighthouse and build a new one. That lighthouse is still in use. The only time it was dark was on June 2, 1970, when a fire broke out. The light has been replaced several times. The earliest light was fueled by whale oil. Later, kerosene was used. Today, the light is electric. The Alcatraz lighthouse is the oldest continually operating lighthouse on the West Coast.

The Civil War

As all these changes took place at Alcatraz, on the opposite side of the country, trouble was brewing

A new lighthouse was completed at Alcatraz in 1909.

between the Northern and Southern states. The Southern states wanted to secede, or leave, the Union over the issue of their right to own slaves. Finally in 1861, war broke out, and several Southern states left the Union to form the Confederate States of America.

Although California was far away from the conflict, emotions ran high. Alcatraz was the only permanent military fort on the West Coast. Work continued to strengthen the fortifications, and some of the wooden gun platforms were replaced with granite ones.

These extra precautions were taken because of the fact that San Francisco had a large reserve of gold and silver stored at the United States Mint there. The

United States feared that people sympathetic to the South might try to seize the money to help finance the Confederate cause. United States Army leaders also feared that pro-Southern partisans might attack the arsenal at Benicia, near San Francisco, to capture arms and ammunition.

An underground group called the Knights of the Golden Circle plotted to establish a "Confederate Republic of the Pacific." The group included many California residents who were originally from the South. They approached the local army commander and commander of Alcatraz, Colonel Albert Sidney Johnston, who was a Southerner, to see if he might help. They believed rumors that he was going to allow Southern sympathizers to capture the fort. Although his sympathies were with the Confederacy, Johnston remained faithful to his duties as a United States Army officer. He vowed that he would protect the property of the United States. The Knights of the Golden Circle dropped their conspiracy. Later, Johnston returned to the South, where he became a famous Confederate general. He was killed at the Battle of Shiloh.[5]

Although the guns on Alcatraz were never actually fired in battle during the Civil War, they were called upon three times to stop suspicious ships.

In March 1863, the sailing ship *J. M. Chapman* was stopped by the navy ship *Cyane* and forced to land at

Alcatraz. The *J. M. Chapman* had been outfitted as a pirate ship by three young men who sympathized with the Confederate cause. The ship was loaded with two small brass cannons, rifles, and fifteen fighting men. The men were all placed in prison on Alcatraz.

The next month, one of Alcatraz's own officers was fired upon as he returned from San Francisco at night in a small boat. When the boat did not answer the sentry's request for identification, the sentry fired a shot through the officer's hat, blowing it off his head and waking the entire island. The officer was not hurt.

On October 1, 1863, the flagship of the British fleet in the Pacific was fired upon as it entered the Golden Gate. Because there was no wind, the ship's flag could not be identified. The ship had not given a salute or signal that it was friendly. When the second shot was fired across the bow of the ship, it finally identified itself as the H.M.S. *Sutleg*.[6]

Prison Beginnings

During the Civil War, the main function of Alcatraz was defense. At the same time, however, the military began to use some of the buildings on the island to house prisoners. On August 27, 1861, the post was made the official military prison for the Pacific area. In 1862 President Abraham Lincoln ordered authorities to arrest citizens who helped the South or who took

During the Civil War, Alcatraz Island (pictured here) was used for defense purposes, as well as a place to house some military prisoners.

part in any activities that could be considered disloyal to the Union. In California, many of those arrested were sent to Alcatraz. During the war, the number of prisoners kept there ranged from fifteen to fifty men. Many were soldiers who had committed crimes such as murder, rape, and theft. Others were civilians and politicians who were suspected of being disloyal to the United States. Some of them were people who had cheered in support of Confederate President Jefferson Davis. Others had taken a more active role to help the

Confederacy, and were imprisoned to prevent them from working against the United States.

Most of the prisoners were kept in the guardhouse, which was in the sally port, a building that served as the first line of defense between the dock and the Citadel. More serious criminals were kept in the basement of the Citadel—sometimes called the "dungeon"—at the top of the island.

The prisoners lived in very grim conditions. There was no running water or heat, and toilets and other sanitary facilities were virtually nonexistent. Prisoners slept on the stone floors. They were bothered by fleas, lice, and bedbugs. Sickness was common.[7]

By the end of 1862, the number of prisoners was so great that they overflowed the basement area and had to be housed in one of the rooms where guns were to be mounted. This threatened the security of the fort. To improve conditions, a small, temporary prison was built in 1863 near the sally port. The building measured twenty feet by fifty feet and had three rooms. Two rooms were for sleeping, and the third was a kitchen. The iron bars on the walls made the building into a prison. The prisoners were expected to work under the supervision of an armed guard. If they refused to work, they were put on a diet of bread and water and placed in a "sweat box." This was an area so small that the prisoner could barely stand up.[8]

During the Civil War, the sally port and guardhouse were remodeled to house prisoners. After the war, the new prison was used for military convicts.

When news of President Lincoln's assassination reached California on April 15, 1865, after the Union had won the war, some people cheered. Those who were grieving for the president turned on them in anger. California government officials were worried that there might be rioting and turned to the military for help. An order was issued that anyone cheering the death of the president should be arrested. In all, sixty-eight men were arrested. Thirty-nine of them were sent to Alcatraz, where they were put to work breaking up rocks.[9]

After the Civil War ended, work continued on improving the fortifications. As the years passed, the brick and concrete fortifications were becoming dated. Ships were becoming more and more powerful, and an island defense seemed obsolete.

Although the number of prisoners in the years immediately after the war averaged only twenty, the idea of making Alcatraz into a prison remained. The army recognized that the cold water and swift currents of the bay made escape almost impossible. In the thirty years after the Civil War, three more buildings were erected to house up to one hundred fifty army prisoners. Gradually, Alcatraz was changing from a fort into a prison compound.[10]

ALCATRAZ MILITARY PRISON

As the Civil War ended, military officials realized that Alcatraz had serious shortcomings for defense. The war had brought advances in artillery. Newly designed long-range cannons and rifles would be able to hit and possibly demolish the island's masonry walls. Army engineers began developing plans to improve the island's defensive capabilities.

Major George Mendell of the Corps of Engineers was given the task of redesigning Alcatraz. He recommended leveling the peaks and slopes of the island and fortifying the island with guns and rifles protected by the rocks and dirt that would result from the demolition. He believed the sand and soil would be better for absorbing the impact of enemy missiles. Much of the work would be done by military prisoners. In 1869, Mendell was ready to begin, using some of the less dangerous prisoners to do the work. Those who earned good reputations as workers would have their sentences reduced. There were approximately one hundred military prisoners at Alcatraz at that time. About half of them were used in the work. They used picks, shovels, and wheelbarrows to remove thousands of cubic yards of stone from the cliffs.[1]

Life on Alcatraz

While the military prisoners toiled away reshaping the island, life for the soldiers stationed there and their families was pleasant. In the morning the children attended school; in the afternoon the soldiers had an opportunity to take classes. In 1873 a hospital was

Electrically operated sirens were among the modern additions made to the military prison.

built, and a surgeon was assigned to take care of the health of the people on the island. A formal garden with roses was built near the Citadel. Three Victorian homes for senior officers were built nearby, and the Citadel was remodeled into junior officers' quarters.

The soldiers followed a routine of daily exercises, marching drills, target practice, dress parades, and inspections. In their spare time, they were entertained by concerts, dances, and other social events.[2]

Life for the prisoners was less pleasant. A new cell house had been built of brick. This building had small individual cells that measured three and a half feet by six feet. The cells were stacked in two tiers. Each cell had a sturdy wooden door. The prisoners slept on the floor. As the number of prisoners increased, more wings were added to the prison. In the 1870s, the prisoners built a two-story workshop and recreation hall. A library was opened for both prisoners and soldiers.

Prisoners woke at 5:00 A.M. and were taken to a long mess hall, where they ate breakfast. After breakfast they had a short time for bathing and using a primitive toilet built over the waters of the bay. The more trustworthy inmates were then split up into groups and led to work breaking up rocks. Some were sent to other military forts around the bay. Some of the men were not considered trustworthy enough to work outdoors. These prisoners were given jobs in a small tailor shop or were kept in the cell blocks.

Some prisoners were given extra punishments as part of the penalty for their original crimes. They would be chained to twelve-pound iron cannonballs, which they had to drag around when they walked. The men called this punishment "carrying the baby." Other prisoners were branded on their hips. The letters *D* or *T. D.* stood for desertion, or leaving their group without permission; *T* stood for theft. Sometimes, the guards would beat the prisoners as a punishment.[3]

Reshaping the island continued between 1870 and 1890, even though funds were scarce. Eventually, prisoners would reduce the height of the island from one hundred twenty-five feet to sixty feet, using only hand tools such as picks and shovels.

Who Were the Prisoners?

In the nineteenth century, the army grouped the prison population into two categories: general and military. General prisoners were soldiers who had committed lesser crimes such as desertion or stealing. After serving their sentences, they were usually sent back to regular duty. Military convicts, on the other hand, were inmates who had been found guilty of rape, assault, or murder. When they completed their sentences, they were given a dishonorable discharge. Then they were released with just a suit of clothes and five dollars in cash.

Looking at some of the more dangerous inmates and their punishments gives an idea of the kind of prisoners who were considered a problem. Napoleon Labeare was in prison for deserting his regiment without permission. He was sentenced to five years of hard labor at Alcatraz and forced to wear a ball-and-chain. When he refused to work and then used obscene language in speaking to a guard, he was sent to the "dungeon" for four days.[4]

Charles Camp was another deserter who refused to work. He was placed in a cell and given only water and bread to eat. When he got out, he was sent back to work breaking up rocks. Again, he refused to work. He was sent to the dungeon for seven more days. When he was later reported for being filthy, he was forcibly washed with a hose.[5]

Escape

Although the currents of the cold waters of the bay made escape from Alcatraz difficult, a few of the military prisoners did manage to get away. Occasionally, groups of prisoners would be sent to work on the mainland. In 1879 inmate James Wright escaped from a work party that had been sent to San Francisco. He was later found in a hotel room. He was arrested and taken to the Presidio of San Francisco. He escaped again and was not found.[6]

In May 1878 two prisoners escaped by boat. Then in 1884, another group of prisoners stole a boat belonging to the engineers and escaped. A short time later, two more prisoners escaped. After eating breakfast at 5:30 A.M., they sneaked to the dock, stole a boat belonging to one of the engineers, and pulled away from shore. A sentry saw them but did not shoot because he thought a passing steamer, the *Sonoma*, would recapture them. The *Sonoma* did chase the men, but the men were able to get to shore and disappear.

In 1906 four prisoners tried to escape by floating off in a butter vat they had stolen from the bakery. The winds and currents made them turn back. When they reached Alcatraz again, they hid in a powder magazine until they were discovered.[7]

The last part of the nineteenth century was a time when the army fought American Indians in the plains and deserts of the West over land disputes. When they were captured, the Indian warriors were confined on Alcatraz. The first American Indian prisoner was known as Paiute Tom. He arrived from Nevada on June 5, 1873, and was killed by a guard two days later. It was believed that he was trying to escape.

Bronco and Sloluck were warriors of the Modoc tribe of northeastern California, which had fought a war against the United States. The two were sentenced to death for murdering Brigadier General E. R. S. Canby in 1873. Their sentences were later changed to life in prison. Bronco died at Alcatraz in 1875 and was buried on nearby Angel Island. Sloluck was transferred to Fort Leavenworth, Kansas.[8]

War, Earthquake, and Fire

On April 24, 1898, Spain declared war on the United States over Cuban independence. The United States wanted Cuba to become independent from Spain because American business investments there were estimated at $50 million. Trade with Cuban ports amounted to around $100 million yearly. The war, which only lasted eight months, took place on two fronts—in the Caribbean and in the Pacific around the Philippines, which was also dominated by Spain.

As American soldiers returned from the Pacific, many were suffering from tropical diseases. A wing was built onto the Alcatraz fort hospital to house these soldiers while they recuperated. Soldiers who had been convicted of military offenses while on duty in the Pacific were also brought to the island. As a result, the number of inmates rose dramatically. In the summer of 1899, there was an average of twenty-five prisoners housed on the island. Ten months later, there were four hundred forty-four prisoners. Some officers suggested that a modern military prison was needed in the West, and they believed that Alcatraz would be an ideal spot. Others argued that the island should continue to be a fortress for defense.

In 1906 a dramatic event occurred that emphasized the importance of using Alcatraz Island as a prison. At 5:30 A.M. on April 18, 1906, a severe earthquake shook San Francisco and the surrounding towns, causing many buildings to collapse. Under the streets of San Francisco, gas lines broke, causing a fire that raged throughout the city, destroying homes and buildings. The flames turned into a firestorm that caused buildings

SOURCE DOCUMENT

After the Spanish-American War of 1898, federal officials decided to use Alcatraz solely as a military prison. This sketch shows the layout of the prison buildings as they looked around 1905.

to explode and asphalt streets to burn. By the next day, the fire was approaching the city jail. It was decided to move the 176 prisoners being held there to Fort Mason on the waterfront. Later the same day, the prisoners were herded onto a boat that took them the short distance to Alcatraz. Although the cell blocks were already full, the military prisoners had to make room for the civilian inmates who included thieves, muggers, drug addicts, and drunks from the city.[9]

In a way, this marked the beginning of a new era for Alcatraz. In 1909 Alcatraz became the United States Military Prison, Pacific Branch, Alcatraz Island. A new, reinforced concrete prison was built on the site of the barracks that had been built in 1858. Construction was completed in 1912.

A New Prison

In order to build the new prison, the army decided to tear down the three-story Citadel that stood at the top of the island. One level of the old building remained. This was the lowest floor, which had held kitchens and servants' rooms. This level was to serve as the basement of the new prison building. The many small rooms would be used for solitary confinement. One wing of the new prison would have a hospital, kitchen, mess hall, barbershop, and work rooms. An exercise yard was built, surrounded by a fifteen-foot wall. The new prison was made of top-grade concrete. Riveted steel bars were placed on all cell doors. The original granite doors were salvaged from the Citadel to be used at the entrance of the new building.

In the early 1920s, a tunnel on the east side of the stockade was made into a morgue where those who died in the prison were kept until they were released for burial. There was a table for autopsies and three refrigerated vaults for the storage of bodies.[10]

New Ideas About the Role of Prisons

In the early twentieth century, prison officials were beginning to change their ideas about the treatment of inmates. They believed that harsh punishment did not work to reduce crime. Many thought the prison's goal should be the rehabilitation of prisoners rather than just punishment. Rehabilitation refers to educating inmates so that they will be able to change their criminal behavior. The new theories began to influence programs at prisons across the United States, including Alcatraz.

In 1915 the prison at Alcatraz got a new name that reflected these ideas: Pacific Branch, United States Disciplinary Barracks. A special school was set up at Alcatraz to give the military prisoners training. The school had three departments. One had graded school education, with classes that included Spanish, arithmetic, reading, geography, and grammar. A second school offered vocational training to help the men get jobs when they were released from prison. The third school provided military training for soldiers who would return to regular service when they finished their prison terms.[11]

One former prisoner wrote back to a prison official:

Dear Sir,

I have the pleasure in writing you a few lines to let you know that I am well and working everyday and making twenty-five dollars a week. I arrived home Monday night at 6:25 P.M. and Tuesday I got a job as an automobile mechanic and am doing fine. They all like me at the garage and I am on my way for advancement which I am in hopes to secure in about five weeks if nothing happens.[12]

Most of the approximately five hundred inmates were young soldiers between the ages of twenty-one and twenty-five. Most were in prison for disciplinary reasons. There were also a few others, called conscientious objectors, who, for religious reasons, refused to fight in World War I, which the United States entered in 1917.

The National Civic Liberty Bureau protested to the War Department over the treatment of the conscientious objectors. They said that some of these young men had been forced to stay in cages that were only fourteen inches deep and fourteen inches wide. They said that some of the men had been kept in the cages for as long as ten days and had collapsed when they were released. The military officers in charge of Alcatraz answered, "Prisoners are only sentenced to the iron cages when they positively refuse to work."[13]

In addition to the prisoners, there were a number of families who lived on Alcatraz. They were the families of the guards and military personnel who worked at the prison. Some trustworthy prisoners worked for the families, taking care of children. Some were servants, and others served as valets for the military officers. The small amount they earned was held in trust for them.

Every morning, the children of these families would take a boat ride from Alcatraz Island to Fort Mason in San Francisco, where they were met by a government bus that took them to school. Back home on the island, in their spare time, they would play hide-and-seek around the abandoned fortifications. In the 1920s, movies were a popular form of entertainment. On Wednesday and Sunday nights, families would often join the prisoners in the cell house to watch the latest films.

Friday night boxing matches between inmates were also popular. A boxing ring would be set up in the dining hall. Soldiers and officers from the mainland would come by boat to watch the matches. For the last match, several blindfolded prisoners would fight one another all at the same time. According to tradition, the convicts chosen to fight were those who had ongoing grudges against each other.[14]

Public curiosity about Alcatraz continued because the island was off-limits to the public. There were rumors that secret Spanish dungeons were carved in the rock under the cell block. Many people believed the island prison was escape-proof. Some reporters began to call Alcatraz "Uncle Sam's Devil Island." Devil's Island was a famous French prison colony on an island off the shores of South America. The name would stick when Alcatraz became a federal prison in 1934.

5

FEDERAL PRISON

During the last ten years that Alcatraz was used by the military, the army became concerned with the great expense of maintaining the prison. There were also concerns that the island prison's reputation was hurting the image of the army. As early as 1913, claims were made that the prison gave an unfair impression of army discipline. Finally, the army reached a decision and announced that the military prison would be closed in 1933.[1]

The United States Department of Justice looked at the possibility of using the island as a federal penitentiary, or prison. J. Edgar Hoover, the director of the Federal Bureau of Investigation (FBI), wanted a super prison to hold the toughest criminals in the country. The nation was experiencing a crime epidemic, partly due to Prohibition.

Prohibition and Crime

For almost fourteen years between 1920 and 1933, the manufacture, transportation, and sale of alcoholic beverages was illegal in the United States. The

Eighteenth Amendment to the Constitution, outlawing alcoholic drinks, was passed by Congress in 1917. By 1919 it had been approved by the states and became law. Soon, new illegal sources of liquor became available. Illegal saloons called speakeasies appeared in every city. Bootlegging—the illegal manufacturing and selling of liquor—became a big business. Transporting liquor from one state to another was a federal crime. Big-time crime and organized gangsters became involved in the new illegal businesses.[2]

During the same period, other gangs of criminals robbed mail trucks, trains, and post offices. Robbing mail is a federal offense. Some bootleggers and bank robbers such as "Machine Gun" Kelly, Harvey Bailey, and Albert Bates and the Karpis-Barker gang turned to kidnapping for ransom. If the kidnappers crossed state lines, they, too, were committing a federal crime.

Many of these Prohibition-era criminals also had reputations for escaping from prison. Sometimes the escapes involved smuggling weapons into prison, killing guards, and shooting their way out of prison. One inmate, John Dillinger, planned the escape of ten prisoners from Indiana State Prison. Taking the warden hostage, Harvey Bailey and Wilbur Underhill escaped from Lansing Prison. In 1933 a carful of gangsters from Kansas City tried to free Frank Nash, who was being returned to prison.[3]

Even though many did not support Prohibition, the public demanded that something be done about the rise in dangerous crime. The attorney general of the United States, Homer Cummings, had heard about Alcatraz and the difficulty of escape from the island. The idea of a federal prison on the island appealed to him.

Federal prisons were fairly new. They hold inmates who are convicted of federal offenses. The first federal prison opened in 1895 at Leavenworth, Kansas. Prohibition added many inmates to the federal prison population, which created new problems. Many prisons became overcrowded. Atlanta Penitentiary had been built to hold two thousand inmates. By the late 1920s, it was crowded with twice that number. In 1929 after a series of riots had occurred, Congress passed laws reorganizing the Federal Prison Bureau. Sanford Bates became its first director.[4]

In 1933 the federal prison system was made up of five penitentiaries, five reformatories, seven correctional prisons, nine prison camps, two reform schools for juveniles, a medical center, and a headquarters. In the early 1930s, there were more prisoners than could fit in these prisons. To make matters worse, prison riots, escapes, and scandals were not unusual. Some of these problems were caused by hard-core troublemakers. It was believed that putting these inmates into a super-high-security prison would improve conditions in the other prisons.

The federal government decided to invest $260,000 in improvements to make Alcatraz escape-proof. The prison would be the final stop for those prisoners who were considered troublemakers in other institutions. They would be cut off from the rest of society. There would be little attempt to reform these prisoners.[5]

The citizens of San Francisco were understandably alarmed when they found out that the nation's most dangerous criminals would be imprisoned a mere mile and a half away on Alcatraz Island. In 1933 the *San Francisco Chronicle* ran editorials and letters opposing the proposed federal prison. The president of the Chamber of Commerce, J. W. Malliard, Jr., said, "I don't think an influx of such prisoners is at all desirable." The chief of police, the Police Commission, and the Board of Supervisors expressed the public's fear that dangerous prisoners might escape to the California mainland.[6]

In spite of the protests, plans continued for improving the prison's security to make it ready for the first shipment of inmates in the summer of 1934.

Warden James A. Johnston

One of the first and most important tasks of the Justice Department in setting up the new prison was choosing a man to be in charge. The job of warden went to Californian James A. Johnston, who had been warden in two of California's high-security state prisons. While at Folsom Prison, he did away with the beating of inmates, and he changed the striped uniform that had identified men as prisoners. At the state's toughest prison, San Quentin, he introduced individual treatment of prisoners and allowed prisoners outside the prison walls when building highways. He also tried to reform the inmates through religious instruction. He had invited famous entertainers of the day to come to the prison. Under his leadership, the prison got a library and regular movie shows. He was known as a tough but fair man who believed in rehabilitation and reform rather than just punishment. At Alcatraz, he would turn out to be a stern warden.

When Johnston arrived at Alcatraz on January 2, 1934, he explored the island to see how security could be improved. He later wrote,

> Hour after hour, day after day, I walked back and forth, up and down and around the island, from the dock to the administration building, from the office to the power house, power house to shops, shops to barracks, into the basements, up on the roofs, across the yards, through the tunnels.[7]

Johnston sent his suggestions to Washington, D.C. He decided to keep the solid main prison building that had been built in 1909 and make it more secure. The soft steel cell fronts were replaced with hardened steel. Prisoners were to be housed in one-man cells built in tiers or levels. Across the east and west ends of the building, galleries were built so that armed guards could watch the prisoners' every move.[8]

Each cell was eight feet long and five feet wide. Each had a cot, washstand, and toilet. The cell block was painted in cheerful colors with dabs of shocking pink and bright red.

Cell block D was to be known as the "treatment unit," where difficult prisoners who broke the rules would be separated from other inmates. The cells in D block did not have beds. At night the prisoners were given a mattress to sleep on. In the same block, cells called "holes" were built to punish inmates who broke serious rules. The "holes" used solid doors, rather than bars, to block out all light and confine the prisoners.

High guard towers were placed around the island. One overlooked the dock. Another rose over the road near the yard wall. A third was on the administration building. Another was at the back of the power house. Armed guards in each kept a twenty-four-hour watch.

At the main entrance, Johnston stationed two guards who worked together to let people in and out. Visitors were visually examined by the guard in the armory. If the visitor passed inspection, the guard would press a lever that removed a protective shield from the lock. The second guard would then open the door with a key. Then the shield would slide back over the lock. In order to pass into the cell house, the visitor had to go through two more doors, one of solid steel and the other made of steel bars. Anyone wishing to leave had to go through the process once again.

Metal detectors were placed at the landing dock, the visitors' entrance, the door to the cells, and the exit to the workshops. Johnston wanted to make sure that knives or guns would not get into prisoners' hands.

Armed guards stationed in the towers watched over the prison twenty-four hours a day.

Rules and Regulations

Warden Johnston wanted to make sure that Alcatraz had maximum security. Knowing that the inmates from other federal prisons would be troublemakers, he set strict rules. To reinforce their feelings of isolation, prisoners could not have newspapers or radios. Only one visitor a month was allowed, and this had to be a relative. The visit could only last for two hours, and the prisoner was separated from the visitor by a thick panel of shatterproof glass. They spoke through telephones and could not discuss current events. Conversations could only be about family matters. Guards listened in and would cut the telephone connection if this rule were broken. Prisoners' mail was censored, and prisoners could only receive packages containing personal items. To keep them from receiving letters with coded or invisible messages, prisoners did not receive the original letters, but copies typed by Alcatraz staff. This also kept the prisoners from receiving mail that might contain paper that had been soaked with narcotics.

To keep escape attempts at a minimum, Alcatraz had a rule of silence. Prisoners were not to speak to one another in the cell block or dining hall. Prisoners were locked in their cells for fourteen hours a day, seven days a week. They could not have any money,

The metal detector at Alcatraz was considered high technology. Prisoners had to pass through the detector an average of eight times a day.

and as there was no prison store, they could not buy personal items like candy or soap.

In many prisons, inmates received rewards for good behavior. At Alcatraz, inmates did not have this kind of encouragement. Punishment for bad behavior might mean being put in the "hole," being placed on a diet of bread and water, and having a loss of "good time." "Good time" meant reducing a prisoner's sentence by ten days for every thirty days he had good behavior.[9]

Alcatraz had the reputation of being a clean, quiet, and orderly prison. In 1937 one inmate wrote to his brother describing his impression of the prison: "The living conditions are better here than in any other institution in which I've been. The cell house is clean, so clean that the floors reflect light. They are of concrete; literally they are being cleaned continuously that they are polished until they show reflection."[10]

Selecting a Staff

Johnston knew that he had to select a staff of guards to help him run the new prison. He also wanted to have a large number of officers to guard America's most dangerous criminals. There would be one guard to every three prisoners, far more than at any other prison, where the usual number was one guard for every seven inmates.

Although being a prison guard was not the most popular occupation, Johnston did not have a difficult time finding the right men. In 1934 the United States was in the middle of the Great Depression, a time when many people were unemployed. Federal prison officers were highly paid. The starting salary was $3,000 a year, compared with $2,400 earned by prison officers in the state of Maryland. By 1963, a guard at Alcatraz received a starting salary of $4,830 with the possibility of earning up to $5,820. For its time, this was a relatively high wage.[11]

Johnston was allowed to hire staff from other penitentiaries. When the prison first opened, there were fifty-two correctional officers.[12] Because the inmates were criminals who might stop at nothing in order to escape, the guards had to go through a demanding training course that included gymnastics, marching, drilling, boxing, wrestling, jujitsu, and the use of weapons such as gas and firearms. They were also trained in sociology, psychology, and criminology to help them understand the criminal mind. They took part in role-playing exercises to teach them how to react in dealing with inmates. Johnston organized the guards into three shifts, each of which was given a color code. Day-yellow worked from 7:00 A.M. to 5:00 P.M. Night-red worked from 5:00 P.M. to midnight. Morning-green worked from midnight to 7:00 A.M.[13]

The Prisoners Arrive

Public interest in the new prison was high because many people were fascinated by the criminals whose stories were making front-page headlines. Early in 1934 the *San Francisco Chronicle* reported that mobster Al Capone and kidnapper "Machine Gun" Kelly would be among the first inmates to be sent to the new prison. Warden Johnston and other prison officials refused to let the press know the names of the inmates being brought to Alcatraz. The lack of information increased public fascination with the prison. The secrecy would continue throughout the years that Alcatraz served as a federal prison. Reporters were not invited to the island to get a firsthand look at the prison. Like the public, their only view of the island was through the telescopes set up at Fisherman's Wharf. Secrecy added to the mystery that surrounded Alcatraz.

Finally, the prison was ready for occupancy. On August 2, 1934, Robert Bradford Moxon arrived. Moxon was of special interest to the public because earlier he had served as a soldier on Alcatraz when it had been a disciplinary barracks. He had been convicted of writing bad checks. When he broke probation, he was sent to McNeil Island in Washington State. From there, he was sent to Alcatraz. When he arrived at the island where he had served in the military, he is reported to have said, "[T]hey've sure changed this joint."[14]

Unlike Moxon, the first prisoners were hard-core inmates who had stirred up riots and planned escapes at other federal penitentiaries. There would also be gangsters like Al Capone who had continued to run their illegal businesses even while they were in prison.

On the evening of August 18, 1934, certain inmates at Atlanta Penitentiary were handcuffed and shackled with leg irons and loaded onto a heavily fortified six-car train for the three-and-a-half-day trip across the country.

In spite of the secrecy, on August 22, when the train finally pulled into Tiburon across the bay from Alcatraz, there were about two hundred people waiting by the tracks. In the water offshore, reporters and cameramen were onboard a boat. The prisoners' cars were loaded onto a barge with rails. Guarded by a Coast Guard ship that had armed officers onboard, the barge was pulled by a tugboat across the water to Alcatraz.

The prisoners' leg irons were removed when the barge docked, but they remained handcuffed. They were herded off the barge and forced to walk between two files of Alcatraz guards up the steep hill to the prison compound. Warden Johnston was seated at a desk near the back entrance. As he called out the names of the inmates, they came in and had their handcuffs removed. Atlanta warden Arthur C. Alderhold, who had accompanied the prisoners on the train, turned their papers over to the deputy, or assistant warden of Alcatraz, who then assigned them new prison numbers.

Afterward, the prisoners were stripped and their body cavities were searched for illegal items such as drugs or coiled watch springs, which could be straightened and made into a saw or a weapon. They were issued prison uniforms. The weekday uniform consisted of gray denim pants and a shirt. The Sunday uniform was blue denim. The front and back of each uniform had the prisoner's number stamped in large digits. The prisoners were also issued sheets, a pillowcase, a towel, a comb, and a toothbrush. They were then taken to their cells.

When the operation was completed, Warden Johnston sent a telegram to Attorney General Homer Cummings. It read, "FIFTY-THREE CRATES FURNITURE FROM ATLANTA RECEIVED IN GOOD CONDITION INSTALLED NO BREAKAGE."[15]

The new prison was open.

★ 6 ★

PRISON LIFE

It was not long before the new prisoners were joined by a second trainload of prisoners from the Midwest. The second group left Leavenworth Penitentiary in Kansas on Saturday, September 1, 1934. As with the first trainload, security was very high. There were rumors that gangs near Kansas City would try to capture the train and free the prisoners, but the train arrived at Richmond, a city on the bay across from San Francisco, at 6:00 A.M. on September 4.[1]

As before, Warden Johnston refused to tell the press and the public the names of the new arrivals, but it soon leaked out that the second shipment included notorious bank robbers and kidnappers Harvey Bailey and "Machine Gun" Kelly, and Roy Gardner, a mail-train bandit. These names were familiar to everyone at the time because their crimes had been headline news. Prison staff worked very hard to establish strict rules so that these and other famous inmates would be treated the same as less famous inmates. On Alcatraz, all inmates were equal, and no one was to receive special advantages.

The prisoners lived in small barred cells that were on three levels, or tiers. Until 1940, the rows of cells were called A block, B block, and C block. Prisoners gave names to the aisles that ran between the cell blocks. The aisle between A and B blocks was called Michigan Boulevard. Broadway was the name of the aisle between B and C blocks, the main pathway leading

Prisoners lived in small cells that had reinforced iron bars. The cells were arranged in levels, one above the other. Inmates called the bottom level "the flats." The two levels above them were called "tiers."

to the dining area. The space in front of the dining area was called Times Square.[2]

Prison Life

The new inmates found that life on Alcatraz was marked by monotony and routine that often broke the men's spirits. Warden Johnston had been given the job of creating a prison system that would defy escape and disorder. He did this through strict rules and a schedule that rarely varied.

The day began early. All prisoners were awakened at 6:30 A.M. by the loud blast of the cell-house alarm clock. They had twenty minutes to get ready before the day's first head count. They made their beds, tidied up their personal items, cleaned the wash basin and toilet, wiped off the bars, swept the prison floor, folded up the table and seat, and then got dressed. At 6:50 A.M., the inmates stood at the doors of their cells for the morning head count. When the count was completed, the lieutenant of the guards ordered the electronically controlled locks on the cells to be released. Then the prisoners were marched to the dining hall for breakfast. A typical breakfast might be oatmeal, coffee, and coffee cake. Twenty minutes were allowed for eating. Conversation was not allowed. Inmates hated the rule of strict silence in the mess hall. Prison officials believed that the rule of silence was necessary because in other prisons inmates would hatch plans for riots and other disturbances at mealtime.³ When they finished breakfast, the inmates had to place their knives, forks, and spoons on their trays. The knife was placed at the left, the fork in the center, and the spoon on the right. A guard would inspect the tables to make sure that all the silverware was in the proper place so that it

A cell contained an iron bed, shelf, wash basin, and toilet.

could be counted and picked up to assure it was not removed from the room.

At 7:20 A.M., some of the prisoners would go to the recreation yard. Others would go to work or return to their cells. Those who were assigned to the shop were counted by the foreman, who then called the head count to the lieutenant of the watch. At 9:30 A.M., the men had a ten-minute rest break during which they could smoke, but not gather in groups. They were then recounted and returned to work. Head counts were taken regularly throughout the day to make sure all prisoners were accounted for.

At 11:40 A.M., the main meal of the day was served, followed by more head counts. In the afternoon, the inmates returned to work. The evening meal was served at 4:25 P.M. Prisoners then spent the evenings in their cells. At 9:30 P.M., lights in the cells were turned off.[4]

Religious services provided a little bit of a break in the monotony. On alternating Sundays, Catholic or Protestant services were offered. Jewish inmates had services on Saturday. Inmates who attended religious services were penalized by losing an hour from their recreation.[5]

On Sunday afternoons the men were allowed two hours in the yard unless they had attended church services. Then they were only allowed one hour outside.

On holidays, time passed pretty much as usual. However, if Christmas and New Year's Day did not fall on a Sunday, prisoners got an extra Sunday schedule for the holidays.

In 1936, when the first inmates were released from Alcatraz on parole, stories began to circulate about the effects of the monotonous routine on prisoners. Bryan Conway, one of the first convicts to be released, said, "Men slowly go insane under the exquisite torture of routine." On his release in 1936, Al Loomis, a counterfeiter and former boxer, told the United Press that a

SOURCE DOCUMENT

A sign posted at the prison barbershop gave a list of the strict rules prisoners had to follow in regard to their appearance. Razor blades were monitored to keep inmates from using them as weapons.

suicide watch was kept whenever a prisoner shaved. He said that twice a week an inmate was given a dull razor blade. He had to shave in two minutes while a guard watched to make sure he would not try to commit suicide. Loomis said, "Many almost succeeded by slashing legs and arms. It's hell there. Life gets so monotonous you feel like bucking the rules to break the monotony. That's it—the monotony. It's driving the men screwy."[6]

Among the most hated rules were the regulations about mail. Inmates were allowed to write letters only to their immediate relatives. Each prisoner would be given three sheets of lined paper. He could write on only one side, and his full name and number had to appear on each page. Any person he wrote about had to be referred to by his or her full name; nicknames were not allowed. The letters were then given to the guard to be mailed. Any letter to the prisoner's attorney had to be approved by a prison officer.[7] All mail was censored to keep prisoners from planning escape attempts.

There were also strict visitation rules. Visitors were restricted to an inmate's wife, parents, brothers and sisters, and children. When gangster Al Capone first arrived, he requested a visit with the warden and told him that he expected to have a lot of visitors. At other prisons, Capone had continued to control his gang from inside prison, communicating through letters and visits. He was told that at Alcatraz, the rules applying to the other prisoners would also apply to him.[8]

Mealtime was a bright spot in a prisoner's life. Food was fairly good, compared with that served in other prisons at the time. There was a wide variety:

SOURCE DOCUMENT

INSTITUTION
RULES & REGULATIONS

UNITED STATES PENITENTIARY
ALCATRAZ, CALIFORNIA

PAUL J. MADIGAN
Warden

In the 1950s, prisoners were given a book of rules that spelled out the daily routine of prison life.

Beef, bologna, frankfurters, pork, sausage, bacon, ham, and corned beef were among the foods served.

Checking books out of the library was another small pleasure. The prison library was well stocked with different books. A prisoner could read authors such as Miguel de Cervantes, Daniel Defoe, Jack London, and Zane Grey. He could also read a variety of magazines, though these were censored to remove articles that had sexual content.

Work also offered some relief from monotony. Inmates did laundry and dry cleaning for the military. Welders repaired buoys for the navy. The tailor shop produced trousers for the army.

Hungry for companionship, some inmates made pets out of mice they found in their cells. They made nests in their bathrobe pockets for the mice, and sometimes they would smuggle their pets into the dining hall to feed at the table. One inmate caught flies and beetles to feed a pet lizard he found on the prison grounds.

Inmates also had clever ways to secretly brew liquor in the prison bakery by soaking raisins and other dried fruits in a crock and adding yeast. When this was discovered, they began brewing liquor in the furniture shop.

Prisoners eagerly looked forward to recreation time in the yard. Basketball, shuffleboard, and horseshoes were popular sports. Other inmates liked to sit on the steps and look at the view. To the west, they could see the expanse of the Golden Gate Bridge. To the north, they could see the city of San Francisco. It was a relief from being confined in a cramped cell.[9]

Punishments

With so many rules, it was natural that there would be defiance among inmates who were hardened law-breakers. Punishment for breaking the rules was swift.

A prisoner could take as much food on his plate as he wished, but if he did not eat it all, he would be forced to miss the next meal. Prisoners had to keep complete silence in the dining hall.[10]

During Alcatraz's first three years, the rule of silence applied to much of the prison life. Prisoners were only allowed to talk in the shops during the three-minute morning and afternoon rest periods and in the yard on Sunday afternoon. During this time, however, the guards tried to keep the men apart so that they could not plot riots and escapes. At meals, an inmate could make a short request such as "Pass the sugar." Those who started further conversations were sent to solitary confinement.

In 1937 the rule of silence was loosened. Inmates believed the change came about because one prisoner challenged the rule by talking out during a meal. As a

Prisoners looked forward to Sundays when they could spend a few hours outdoors in the recreation yard.

guard headed toward the inmate to punish him, another inmate spoke out in answer. Within a few moments, everyone was talking. The guards were helpless, because there was not enough room for everyone in the disciplinary cells.

In 1940, the "dungeon" was replaced by D block, which was built to keep prisoners who were being punished by solitary confinement. Some were kept in cells with open fronts, away from the general prison population. For more serious offenses, others were sent to the "hole" for ninety days or longer.[11]

To be sent to D block, a prisoner might have violated one or more of the following rules: Caps could not be worn in the cell house. Although tobacco was readily available to inmates, they could only smoke in their cells, in the library, and in A block. Smoking or carrying a lighted cigarette outside the cell was grounds for punishment. Loud talking, entering another inmate's cell, or possessing forbidden objects such as an extra paper clip or shoelace were cause for discipline. Cigarettes or candy received as gifts had to be used up quickly or would be considered contraband.[12]

In addition to D block, there was psychological torture. After lockup at night, the inmates could hear the guards at target practice. They would sometimes see the targets—bullet-filled dummies wearing prison uniforms—strewn around the yard when they went to work in the shops.

There were other punishments not written in the rule book. A jet of water from a high-pressure hose might be used to control an unruly inmate by knocking the wind out of him. Special handcuffs could be tightened around the wrists, causing pain. Straightjackets were used to confine an inmate's body. These types of punishment, common to many prisons at that time, were not favored by Warden Johnston, so they were used sparingly at Alcatraz.[13]

Although secrecy surrounded the activities on Alcatraz, as men were released, news spread that the new federal prison was crueler than other prisons.

In 1935 an inmate named Verrill Rapp, who had been paroled to stand trial on other charges, spoke to reporters about the inhumane treatment of prisoners on Alcatraz. He said that inmates were going insane.

A rumor spread that as a punishment, some inmates were locked up in Spanish dungeons. In reality, the Spaniards had never done any building on Alcatraz, so, of course, there were no Spanish dungeons. The rooms referred to as dungeons were actually the first floor of the old Citadel, which had become the basement of the prison. In the early years that Alcatraz operated as a federal prison, some prisoners were locked up there.

One inmate wrote, "They used to put leg irons on the men in the dungeon. But most of the cons found ways to slip them off and then throw them out, so the guards quit the leg irons and took to handcuffing the prisoners to the bars."[14]

In the spring of 1941, inmate Henri Young was sent to San Francisco to stand trial in federal court for the murder of another inmate at Alcatraz. His attorneys argued that mistreatment had made him temporarily insane at the time he committed the crime. A number of inmates were brought to the court to testify about the harsh treatment at the prison. They told of long stays in solitary confinement in cells without lights, toilets, or furniture. Once, Young had been kept in total darkness for nineteen days without a bath. Under examination, Warden Johnston admitted that the men in solitary received only one full meal in three days, with bread and water in between. Young's record revealed that he had been placed in solitary confinement for such violations as not eating all his food, having two pairs of socks in his cell, getting into a fistfight in the yard, and banging a pillow on the floor of his cell. The jury found Young guilty of involuntary manslaughter, a lesser offense than murder, and issued a statement to the press saying that conditions at Alcatraz were inhumane.[15]

Other inmates told of beatings by the guards. Those confined to the "hole" had to sleep on the floor with only a blanket to keep out the cold. Rats might run in and out. They told of having no toilet, just a hole in the floor. The only meal might be a few slices of bread at noon. After five years, the use of the basement cells was stopped. When James Bennett, the head of the federal prison system, visited Alcatraz, he told Warden Johnston to use these cells only in an emergency.[16]

Alcatraz was probably no better or worse than other prisons. After Warden Johnston retired in 1949, he wrote a book called *Alcatraz Island Prison and the*

Men Who Live There. He claimed that the inmates there had conditions that were as good or better than at other federal prisons. Some inmates actually wanted to be sent there, partly for protection from violence at other prisons and partly because it gave them an image and reputation for badness.[17]

Kids on Alcatraz

Although the inmates were the most famous residents on Alcatraz, the island was also home to the families of the prison employees. During the summer of 1934, when guards and their families began moving to Alcatraz, the weather broke records as the hottest and driest in the island's history. The families soon learned that living on the island was very different from living on the mainland. The fifty to sixty children who lived on Alcatraz when the prison first opened had more freedom than those who came later when more fences were built to separate the prison from the civilians. Actually, the prison was only a short distance from the staff living quarters.

Contact with inmates was discouraged. Although prisoners were closely guarded, there were times when a prisoner might tip his hat in greeting or toss a ball to a child. One former resident remembered that as a child, he and his friends liked to play handball with a tennis ball that had the fuzz taken off. He said that sometimes the children would throw tennis balls to the inmates working on the dock, who would remove the fuzz for them with a wire power brush in the shop.[18]

Although a sense of danger was present, most of the children were not too affected by it. They rarely saw the inmates. Jolene Babyak, author of *Eyewitness on Alcatraz*, lived on Alcatraz as a child. She was the daughter of a deputy warden. One of her earliest memories was hearing prisoners yelling and dragging their cups on the bars of their cells at night, a way they sometimes welcomed a new inmate. She wrote, "Although my parents never communicated anything as strong as hatred or even dislike for the prisoners, I knew instinctively to keep my distance."[19]

The isolation of living on Alcatraz sometimes made life difficult. Young people had to take the prison boat to the mainland for school. In the early years, the boat made nine round-trips a day. In the 1950s and 1960s, the prison boat, the *Warden Madigan*, made twenty-two round-trips a day. The school boat left at 7:10 A.M. and took twelve minutes to get to San Francisco. Most of the students returned home by 4:10 P.M. At Fort Mason in San Francisco, where the boat docked, a pulley-operated gangplank would move up and down as the tides changed, often making it difficult to get on and off the launch. Families would have to bring everything—groceries, furniture, clothing, books—to the island by boat.

For many years, the last boat to Alcatraz left San Francisco at midnight. In later years, a 2:00 A.M. boat could be requested. That meant that if a teenager missed the midnight boat and asked for the 2:00 A.M. boat, his or her parents would be called.[20]

At Alcatraz, something as commonplace as throwing out garbage was a cause for concern. Because inmates' reading materials were restricted, residents had to bundle up newspapers and magazines for a special Saturday pickup. Anything that might be made into weapons could not be thrown in the trash. Razor blades, saw blades, tools, bottles, glass, and clothing were also specially collected. Razor blades were of particular concern because they could be easily hidden. These were thrown into the bay. Officers could not carry pocketknives, and children could not have toy guns or water pistols because it was feared that prisoners might find and use them in escape attempts.[21]

For security reasons, children were also restricted as to where they could play. They could never play on the docks, in the building hallways, near the prison, or near the ocean. Outdoor play was restricted to the parade ground. Because the steep streets on Alcatraz Island led to the prison compound, there was no place for older kids to ride bicycles.

Teenagers had an especially hard time. One man remembered climbing on the rocks with a friend on the Golden Gate side of the island as a teenager, an area that was off-limits. Officials feared that a guard in the tower might mistake young people for inmates trying to escape. The boys were called to the warden's office and scolded.[22]

Although living on Alcatraz had its problems, many of the guards and their families remembered their lives there with fondness. The community was closely-knit, and lasting friendships were made. A mimeographed newsletter called the *Fog Horn* was published each month. It told of residents' birthdays, promotions, social clubs, and other activities. Residents felt that life on the island was safe from crime. Many families did not bother to lock their doors. Today, former residents continue to keep in touch through the Alcatraz Alumni Association, which has an annual reunion.[23]

7

THE PRISONERS OF ALCATRAZ

During the years that Alcatraz served as a federal penitentiary, some 1,545 men were imprisoned there. Some of them were small-time criminals who had bad judgment. Stealing mail in a post office or crossing state lines while committing a crime was a federal offense. Others were famous convicts whose crimes had made headline news. They were bosses of Mafia-type gangs, kidnappers, and bank robbers. All made up the history and the mystery that surrounds Alcatraz.

Al Capone

The most notorious inmate was Chicago's mobster boss, Alphonse "Scarface" Capone. Few criminals of the 1930s were as famous as Al Capone, Alcatraz prisoner number 85. Capone got his nickname, "Scarface," because he had received an ugly scar on his face in an attack against him early in his criminal career. During Prohibition, Capone controlled the supply of illegal liquor in Chicago. By 1924 it was reported that he was making one hundred thousand dollars a week from his rackets, which included gambling, prostitution, bootlegging, dog racing, dance halls, and nightclubs. Violence was a by-product of these activities. Rival gangs fought one another for control of criminal rackets. Newspapers reported that from 1923 to 1926, there were 135 gang killings in Chicago. Only six men had come to trial for the killings, and of those, only one had been convicted. After years of violence, the gangs finally agreed that Capone was the underworld boss of Chicago. To secure his position, he killed his rivals. To keep people on his side, he gave money to charity and to the poor. Capone seemed to be above the law.

Although Capone had a long criminal record, he spent only one short term in prison before he was arrested on federal charges. Finally, he was convicted of breaking income tax laws, a federal offense. He was fined $37,617 and sentenced for up to ten years in prison. He was sent to Atlanta Penitentiary, where he continued to control his illegal businesses from his cell. He got away with it by bribing guards. To some observers, it appeared that Capone had more control over the prison than the warden did. It was also feared that the members of his gang might be planning an escape attempt to free him from prison. To prevent

Gangster Al "Scarface" Capone was perhaps the most notorious criminal of the 1930s. He was in the first shipment of prisoners to Alcatraz.

this, it was decided that he should be sent to Alcatraz with the first shipment of prisoners.[1]

Although he had received special privileges at Atlanta, Capone was treated like any other inmate at Alcatraz. The strict rules meant that he had little contact with the outside. He was assigned to work in the laundry, a damp and badly ventilated room. There, inmates washed clothing for the military.

Capone became unpopular with other prisoners because he refused to take part in a prison strike. Some inmates decided to get even. In 1935 he was sent to the "hole" because he got into a fight with another inmate who hit him in the face with a wet bundle of laundry. He was then transferred to the bathhouse cleaning team. There, another inmate stabbed him in the back with a pair of scissors snatched from the barbershop. Other attempts were made to kill him.

In 1938 Capone became very ill and was diagnosed with advanced syphilis, a sexually transmitted disease. On February 5, 1938, he began to show signs of confusion, which led to rumors that Alcatraz had driven Capone crazy. After breakfast he returned to the wrong cell. His speech was slurred. For the rest of his stay at Alcatraz, he was kept in the hospital. He was released from Alcatraz on January 6, 1939, and was sent to a new federal prison at Terminal Island near Los Angeles to serve out a separate one-year sentence. He was later transferred to Lewisberg and was finally released. He spent the final years of his life in Miami, Florida, where he died on January 25, 1947.[2]

Alvin "Creepy" Karpis

Alvin Karpis, born Albin Karpowicz, started his criminal career at the age of ten when it is said he stole his first gun. During his teens, he robbed stores and warehouses in Kansas. He was first sentenced to prison at the age of eighteen. While he was an inmate at Lansing, the Kansas State Penitentiary, he met Freddie Barker. Out of prison, the two formed the Karpis-Barker gang and started a crime wave across the Midwest.

Besides robbing stores and banks, the gang also committed two kidnappings. The first involved snatching William Hamm, Jr., the president of the Hamm Brewing Company in Minnesota. The gang demanded a ransom of one hundred thousand dollars, which was paid. The second kidnapping proved to be their downfall. After they kidnapped Edward Bremer, a bank president, they received a ransom of two hundred thousand dollars. The bills, however, were marked, which allowed federal agents to trace the gang. Freddie and his mother, Ma Barker, were killed in Florida, but the agents could not find Karpis. He became known as Public Enemy Number One.

Finally, in 1936, he was arrested in New Orleans and sentenced to Alcatraz.[3] Karpis's nickname, "Creepy," was given to him by federal officials. After spending twenty-five years at Alcatraz, he was transferred to McNeil Island Prison in Washington State. When he was finally released, he was deported to Canada, the

Alvin "Creepy" Karpis was a bank robber, kidnapper, and murderer. After three escapes from other prisons, he was sent to Alcatraz, where he spent twenty-five years.

country of his birth. His book, *On the Rock*, gives his version of life at Alcatraz.

Karpis's bragging made him unpopular with other inmates at Alcatraz. Because he was also ill-tempered and argumentative, he often got into fistfights. An inmate who was at Alcatraz with Karpis said,

> Old "Creepy" came to "the Rock" with a lot of national publicity hanging all over him, like decorations on a Christmas tree. He was a big shot, and he didn't want no one to forget it. "Creepy" had the mind of a ten-year-old kid, and still has. I wouldn't trust "Old Creepy" as far as a kid could throw him.[4]

"Machine Gun" Kelly

In the 1930s, people's attention focused on the crime of kidnapping after the son of Charles Lindbergh, a famous aviator, was snatched from his home and killed. Congress quickly passed new, stricter kidnapping laws. The FBI acted quickly when those laws were broken. Some of the most notorious kidnappers ended up at Alcatraz. One of these was George "Machine Gun" Kelly. Kelly's real surname was Barnes. He had been raised in a well-to-do family in Memphis, Tennessee, and had attended college. Kelly started his criminal career as a bootlegger, which led to his doing time in prison. While at Leavenworth Penitentiary, he became friends with three of the most notorious bank robbers of the time: Harvey Bailey, Frank Nash, and

Albert Bates. When they were released, he and his new friends staged many bank robberies. Kelly used a Thompson submachine gun, which gave him his nickname, "Machine Gun."

The robbers decided to kidnap an Oklahoma oil millionaire named Charles F. Urschel. They demanded a ransom of two hundred thousand dollars. This was considered an enormous amount at that time. They drove Urschel across state lines to Texas, where they hid him at a ranch belonging to Kelly's brother-in-law. The ransom was paid, and Urschel was released. While being held by the gang, however, Urschel had been very observant. He remembered many details about his capture such as the sound of an airplane that regularly passed over the shack where he was confined. Federal agents were able to figure out where he had been hidden, and they were able to arrest most of the gang. Finally, Kelly and his wife, Kate, who had participated in the kidnapping, were arrested in Memphis, Tennessee, in 1933.

Kelly's gang was the first to be tried under the new Lindbergh Law. Under this law, criminals who transported a kidnapping victim over state lines could be punished by the death penalty. Both Kelly and his wife received life in prison. Kelly, Bates, and Bailey were first sent to Leavenworth, then to Alcatraz.[5]

In the harsh routine at Alcatraz, Kelly was a model prisoner. He served as an altar boy, worked in the industrial offices, and in general, behaved himself. In a letter to the director of prisons he wrote,

> Maybe you have asked yourself, how can a man of even ordinary intelligence put up with this kind of life at Alcatraz? What is this life of mine like? To begin with, these five words seem to be written in fire on the walls of my cell—NOTHING CAN BE WORTH THIS.[6]

The Birdman of Alcatraz

Robert Stroud became famous because of the research he did on birds while he was an inmate. When he was a young man, he had worked at construction in Alaska. A dispute with a bartender ended with murder, and Stroud was sentenced to twelve years at McNeil Island Prison. After he was transferred to Leavenworth, he was kept in the maximum-security unit. He began taking correspondence courses. Through the mail, he was able to study mathematics, astronomy, and engineering.

Stroud's intelligence did not keep him out of trouble. In 1916 he stabbed a guard in a fight. Because the crime took place in a federal prison, he was tried in a federal court and found guilty. He was sentenced to death, a sentence later reduced to life in prison in solitary confinement. He was placed in a small cell that was twelve feet long and six feet wide. To pass the time, he began to care for two sparrows he found in the exercise yard. He asked for and received permission to breed canaries in his cell. It is said that he kept up to two hundred birds in his cell. His research made Stroud well-known with bird breeders all over the world. His research led him to find a remedy for septic fever, a disease that affects birds. For prison officials, Stroud's fame created problems. Prisoners were not supposed to have business with the outside world. In 1942 it was decided to transfer him to Alcatraz.[7]

At Alcatraz, Stroud was kept in solitary confinement. Although he was not allowed to have birds in his cell, he did continue his research. Warden Johnston allowed Stroud to subscribe to bird journals and to correspond with many bird lovers throughout the world. The letters were sent through his brother, who served as a go-between. Stroud finished writing a long book on birds in 1939. In 1943 *Stroud's Digest of the Diseases of Birds* was published. The five-hundred-page book, which contained eighty-seven illustrations handdrawn by Stroud, was praised by critics. The book critic of the *Kansas City Star* wrote, "Stroud's book is a digest of bird diseases that is singularly complete and detailed."[8]

Confined to a cell in the isolation wing, Stroud missed his birds and his research activities. He turned to the Alcatraz library, which had a large collection of law books. Many prisoners passed their time studying law in the hope of finding something that would help them get released. Forty-five inmates had been able to improve their sentences after studying law, and twelve had managed to gain their freedom.

Stroud decided to study law. Although his petitions to the federal court were turned down, he continued studying law and the effects of prison on inmates. He then decided to write a history of the federal prison system from the prisoner's point of view. Because he was not allowed to have a typewriter, he wrote the book by hand.[9]

On several occasions, Stroud attempted suicide. In 1955 his biography, *Birdman of Alcatraz*, by Thomas E. Gaddis was published, but he was forbidden to read it because it mentioned crimes, a forbidden topic for reading material at Alcatraz. Later, a copy was smuggled in to him. The book increased his fame. Many bird lovers began to demand that he be released. In 1959, he was sent to the Federal Medical Facility in Springfield, Missouri. After forty-three years in solitary confinement, he was finally allowed to mingle with other inmates. The 1962 movie about his life, *Birdman of Alcatraz*, made Robert Stroud Alcatraz's most famous inmate. Unlike his portrayal in the movie, however, he never kept birds during his stay at Alcatraz.[10]

The Less Famous Inmates of Alcatraz

Most of the prisoners at Alcatraz were not famous. Some had committed relatively minor offenses. Earl Taylor, an accountant, was sentenced to five years there for tax evasion. Another prisoner was serving time for stealing a pig from an American Indian reservation. A military prisoner was sent there for being absent without leave. Another was sent there for assault and for stealing $1.50.[11]

Many, however, were hardened convicts and troublemakers. Others were tough criminals who used their time in prison to improve themselves through self-education. One such prisoner was Rudolph "Dutch" Brandt. Brandt was serving a sentence of twenty-five years for robbing sixty-five thousand dollars from the Detroit Bank in 1936. Earlier, he had served a term for murder. After serving five months at Leavenworth Penitentiary, he was transferred to Alcatraz. While in solitary confinement, he spent his time studying mathematics. In 1950 Harold Bacon, a mathematics professor at Stanford University, received permission to help Brandt study calculus, which Brandt was taking by correspondence from the University of California. Over the following years, Bacon became friends with Brandt, helping him with his studies and talking with him about his life.

DECEMBER 26, 1950

DEAR MR. BACON:

I RECEIVED YOUR LETTER AND ITS SOLUTION OF THE WINEGLASS PROBLEM I AM FAMILIAR WITH THE FORMULA FOR THE VOLUME OF A SPHERICAL SEGMENT OF ONE BASE BUT I'M NOT SURE THAT I COULD HAVE DERIVED STEP BY STEP THE FORMULA FROM IT, AS YOU DID, FOR SOLVING THIS PROBLEM. AS YOU KNOW, IN ORDER TO DERIVE THE EQUATION OF A HARD-TO-UNDERSTAND PROBLEM AS THIS, ONE MUST KNOW BOTH "HOW" AND "WHY." WHEN I HIT UPON THE METHOD OF MULTIPLICATION (USING THE SQUARE OF HALF THE SUM OF THE TWO NUMBERS MINUS THE SQUARE OF HALF THEIR DIFFERENCE) IN 1948, I THOUGHT THAT I HAD A PRACTICAL NEW METHOD FOR MULTIPLYING NUMBERS AND BELIEVED I WOULD BE ABLE TO DESIGN A CALCULATING MACHINE ON THE PRINCIPLE OF THE ABACUS. I STILL THINK THAT I MAY BE ABLE TO DESIGN THIS MACHINE, PROVIDED THAT I AM ALLOWED TO USE THIS METHOD. I AM A TOOL AND DIE MAKER BY TRADE AND HAVE CONSIDERABLE KNOWLEDGE OF TOOL AND DIE DESIGNING.

MY NEW YEAR WISH FOR YOU IS THAT YOUR BOOK WHICH YOU ARE WRITING WILL BE A SUCCESS AND THAT YOU ENJOY GOOD HEALTH.

SINCERELY YOURS,
RUDOLPH BRANDT, NO. 369
ALCATRAZ, CALIFORNIA

Inmate Rudolph Brandt corresponded with Stanford mathematics professor Harold M. Bacon about math problems he was studying. Their friendship by mail continued after Brandt left Alcatraz.

Brandt was determined to master the difficult study of calculus. In April 1951 he wrote to Professor Bacon:

> I got your letter of April 5th and the solution to the problems. I shall study them just as soon as I am able to. Next May 30 it will be five years since I started to study mathematics and I want to learn as much integral calculus as I can for my fifth anniversary. If your time allows, would you please give me the solution of problem 18, page 235?
>
> Yours sincerely,
> Rudolph Brandt, No. 369[12]

Brandt was finally released in 1953. After getting out of prison, he held a job as a tool and die maker for several years. He continued his correspondence with Professor Bacon. When Brandt died a few years later, one of his friends wrote to Bacon: "I've wondered what a man he would of been if he wouldn't have got into troubles. Life is one funny thing. It all depends on how the ball bounces."[13]

8

ESCAPES AND RIOTS

For most inmates, Alcatraz was a place of hopelessness made more intense by the boring routine. Inmates could look through the barred windows to see the sunlight glittering on the waters of the bay. Across the short expanse of water, the tall buildings of San Francisco represented a life of freedom that seemed both nearby and distant. This added to the feeling of hopelessness. Some inmates reacted against the monotony with violence. Others plotted to escape. Guards felt there was a constant danger.

The first disturbance broke out on January 22, 1936, when inmates revolted against the strict rules, especially the regulation requiring silence. As a punishment, about half the inmate population was put on a diet of bread and water. The strike lasted three days, but the rules did not change.

In September 1937, the men in the machine shop dropped their tools and began shouting, "We want to talk. We want newspapers. We want radios." Warden

Johnston gave them half an hour to get back to work. They refused. He then said that if they did not work, they would not be allowed to eat. Those involved were placed on a diet of bread and water. For several days, the inmates continued shouting and banging their tin cups on the bars of their cells and on the concrete walls. Finally, after five days, the strike seemed to have ended. Most of the men, tired of eating just bread and water, agreed to go back to work. The suspected leaders were sent to the "dungeon."

When Burton "Whitey" Phillips, one of the strike leaders, was released from the "dungeon," he seemed sorry about his role in the rebellion. When he went to the dining hall, however, Phillips broke out of the line of inmates and attacked Warden Johnston, beating him in the face and body. It took five guards to pull him away from the warden. Johnston was in the hospital for a week recovering from his injuries. According to an article written in October 1938 by P. F. Reed, a counterfeiter who was in Alcatraz during the riot, Phillips was beaten by guards.[1]

Sometimes, the prisoners' protests were less violent. After the kitchen crew went on strike, they were put in D block, the isolation unit, for punishment. One night, they began to howl. In other parts of the prison, inmates began to answer with howls. Soon, the cell house was filled with the sounds of inmates howling, chanting, and banging tin cups to show their support.

At other times, inmates would stage a phony fight to distract guards from a real fight in another part of the prison.[2] Most of the attacks that occurred in the prison were inmate against inmate. Usually, these were fistfights, but sometimes prisoners attacked one another with knives, metal pipes, a chair, or an iron weight. Knives might be made out of silverware, parts of scissors, pen parts, screwdrivers, and other metal items that inmates would smuggle out of the dining hall or the shops. Inmates also had ways of getting even with guards. One inmate in a solitary cell would throw feces at the guards when they opened the door.[3]

Escape Attempts

Although inmates had successfully escaped from Alcatraz Island when it was a military prison, it was almost impossible to escape from the federal prison. Beefed-up security combined with the icy waters and swift currents of the bay made getting off the island almost impossible. Still, the overwhelming odds against successfully escaping did not discourage some inmates from trying.

The first escape attempt occurred in April 1936. Joseph Bowers was serving a twenty-five-year sentence for stealing $16.63 from a store. Because a local post office was also located in the store, his theft became a federal offense. A guard saw Bowers at the top of a fence on the island's west side lower level where he had been working. When warning shots did not bring Bowers down, the guard fired at his body, wounding him in the side. The fall to the ground killed him.[4]

The fate of the next two prisoners to attempt escape is not known. Theodore Cole, a convicted kidnapper, and Ralph Roe, a bank robber, disappeared from their jobs in the mat shop on a cold, foggy day in December 1937. Roe was serving a ninety-nine-year sentence; Cole's sentence was for fifty years. It was discovered that they had sawed through the shop window bars and escaped through the window. They used a wrench to break through the gate below. Although the prison launch, San Francisco police boats, and the Coast Guard patrolled the area around the island, they found no sign of the inmates. There was a strong tide that day that probably pulled the men out to sea, where they may have drowned. Their bodies were never recovered, and they are still unaccounted for.[5]

On May 23, 1938, a guard was killed when three inmates tried to escape. Prisoners Thomas Limerick, Rufus Franklin, and James Lucas sneaked out of the woodworking shop and escaped to the third floor of the building, where they ran into a guard, Royal C. Cline, whom they beat to death with a hammer. Then, they climbed to the roof, where they tried to overpower the guard in the tower. The guard, Harold Stites, fired at them, hitting Limerick in the head. Limerick looked surprised, smiled, and fell dead. Stites then shot Franklin in both shoulders, causing him to roll down the roof, where he became tangled in barbed wire. Lucas surrendered. Both Lucas and Franklin were convicted of first-degree murder for Cline's death.[6]

January 1939

The next escape attempt also had a tragic end. Early in the morning on January 13, 1939, the shrill blast of the escape siren woke everyone on the island. Five prisoners had managed to break out of the segregation cells of D block, escaping through a window. The bars in the isolation cells of D block were not made of hardened steel. The prisoners had apparently managed to smuggle a tool past the metal detector into their cells. Arthur "Doc" Barker was serving a life sentence for kidnapping. Henri Young was a convicted bank robber. Dale Stamphill, a kidnapper, was another lifer. William Martin was in prison for post office robbery. Rufus McCain had committed kidnapping and bank robbery. The searchlights uncovered the men on the shore. They were trying to tie their clothes together to make a raft. When the guards opened fire, they hit Barker in the thigh and through the right eye. He died an hour later. Stamphill was shot in both legs. When McCain was found he was nearly naked. He was shivering from the cold and was on his knees begging for mercy. Young was found wearing only his underpants.[7] They surrendered and were sent to solitary confinement, where they were kept until November 1940.

When McCain and Young returned to the general prison population, they argued constantly with each other. Finally, in December 1940, Young stabbed and killed McCain while the two men were working in the tailor shop. In the trial that followed, Young's defense was that he could not be held responsible for the murder because the long stay in solitary confinement had changed his judgment. Warden Johnston was called to testify about living conditions at Alcatraz, and seven inmates testified about the treatment of prisoners. The warden admitted that men were sometimes kept in pitch-black cells for months with only one blanket for warmth. They had to sleep on the concrete floor. Young, the defendant, had been kept in total darkness for nineteen days. When he was removed, he was placed in a narrow cell with a solid steel door that kept out the light. In a year's time, he was only allowed out of the cell once for thirty-five minutes. Although the prisoners' claims were not acted upon, their testimony exposed the harshness of life at Alcatraz.[8] Young was convicted of manslaughter, a lesser crime than murder, and had his sentence extended by three years.[9]

A Violent Escape Attempt

During the 1940s, a number of prisoners tried unsuccessfully to escape from the island. The most violent attempt took place on May 2, 1946. The attempt, which involved six men, began with a riot and ended with death.

Bernard Coy, a cold-blooded bank robber, probably put the plan together. When Coy was sentenced to Alcatraz, he declared that no prison would hold him, and that for him murder meant nothing. At 1:40 P.M., Coy was out of his cell, mopping the cell-house floors. Inmate Marvin F. Hubbard pretended to get sick while working in the kitchen. When he saw an unarmed guard, William Miller, approaching the door to the cell blocks to let Hubbard in, Coy sent a signal to D block. In D block, inmate Sam Shockley was waiting to make a disturbance that would draw the attention of a second guard, Dean Burch. As Miller opened the door for Hubbard, Coy jumped him. Hubbard and Coy tied up the officer and threw him into a cell in C block. Although Miller was dazed, he was able to slip the key to the yard off his key ring and hide it in the cell toilet without being seen. The convicts took his key ring.

The prisoners planned to release the other inmates in their gang: Joseph Cretzer, Miran Thompson, and Clarence Carnes, who was only eighteen when he was sent to Alcatraz. They then planned to get weapons from the guard in the gun gallery, let out the rest of the prisoners, storm the guard towers, and take control of the prison.

Using Miller's keys, the inmates released Carnes and Cretzer. In the meantime, Coy stripped to his long underwear so that he could move faster, climbed to Hubbard's shoulders, and pulled himself up to the gun gallery, twelve feet above the floor. From there, he was able to get to the roof, where he pried open the bars of the gun gallery. He waited for Officer Burch to come back. The two men fought, but Coy was able to choke Burch, who became unconscious. Coy grabbed the guard's pistol and twenty rounds of ammunition and dropped them to Cretzer, who was waiting below. Next, they released Miran Thompson from his cell. As other officers came into the cell block area, they were captured and put into the cell with Miller. Finally, nine officers were captured, and chaos broke out in the cell house.[10]

Guards herded the prisoners who were not involved into the yard, where they were guarded first by the Alcatraz guards and later by the United States Marines, who had been sent to Alcatraz when authorities learned of the incident. Some of the inmates were afraid of being caught in the crossfire. Warden Johnston sent a radio message to the Coast Guard and to the San Francisco police, telling them of the trouble and asking them to send patrol boats to circle the island.[11]

The escape attempt began on Thursday, May 2, and it took until Saturday, May 4, for the prison administration to regain control. Officers Stites and Miller were killed. Inmates Bernard Coy, Joseph Cretzer, and Marvin Hubbard also paid with their lives. Samuel Shockley, Miran Thompson, and Clarence Carnes, the remaining inmates involved in the escape attempt,

SOURCE DOCUMENT

The prison riot made headline news in the San Francisco Chronicle *on May 4, 1946.*

were tried and found guilty of murder. Shockley and Thompson were executed in the gas chamber at San Quentin State Prison. Carnes received a second life sentence because of his age.[12] When Alcatraz closed, he was sent to Leavenworth. He was paroled from prison in the late 1970s.[13] In spite of the deaths resulting from this escape attempt, no one managed to escape from Alcatraz.

More Attempts to Escape

In the 1950s, there were two escape attempts. In the first, Floyd P. Wilson, an inmate serving a life sentence for murder, disappeared from a work crew. Although he managed to hide from the guards for almost twelve hours, he was finally recaptured.

The next two prisoners who attempted to escape were somewhat more successful. On September 29, 1958, bank robber Clyde Johnson and post office robber Aaron Burgett, escaped from the garbage crew. They tied the guard to a tree, taping his eyes and mouth shut.

When the escape was discovered, Coast Guard patrols circled the island for two hours. They finally found Johnson, but Burgett was still missing. A nationwide alert was posted. Thirteen days later, his body was found floating in the bay.[14]

Miran Thompson (left), one of the inmates who started the May 1946 riot, was tried for the murder of two guards. He was sentenced to death and on December 3, 1948, was executed at San Quentin Prison in California.

The Most Daring Attempt

The most famous and daring escape attempt occurred on June 11, 1962. To this day, the attempt intrigues the public because no one knows for sure whether or not it was successful. The escape attempt was made famous by San Francisco journalist J. Campbell Bruce in his book, *Escape from Alcatraz*. In 1978 the movie of the same name starred Clint Eastwood as Frank Lee Morris, one of the alleged masterminds of the plot.[15]

Plans for the escape began months earlier by Frank Lee Morris and two brothers, John and Clarence Anglin. The three men were bank robbers who had been in prison together in Atlanta before their transfer to Alcatraz. Their plan displayed tremendous creativity.

To escape from their cells, the men used kitchen utensils to chip away the rotting cement from the ten-by-six-inch ventilation holes at the back of their cells. To replace the missing grills, they made grills out of cardboard, using paint from kits they had been given for artwork. Squeezing through the vent holes, they were able to make a hidden work area above their cells. There, they made life preservers from stolen raincoats. They also made dummy heads using a powder made from a mixture of soap and concrete. Using their fingers and the flat part of a spoon handle, they carved facial features into the heads. They used scraps of hair from the barbershop and the paint from their art kits to make fairly lifelike heads. The dummy heads were placed in their beds so that passing guards would think they were asleep when they were actually at work making preparations for the escape. Sneaking out of their cells through the vents, they worked at spreading the metal bars in the air vents that allowed access to the roof.

After 9:30 P.M. on June 11, they placed the dummy heads in their bunks. They squeezed through the cell-house roof vent and were able to reach the ground below. Climbing over the fifteen-foot fence, they disappeared. After that, no one really knows what happened.[16]

The waters in the bay that night were a chilly 54° F. Visibility was good, which would help the men find their way to the mainland. In the days following the escape, authorities searched for the men. Soldiers from the Presidio of San Francisco looked for them on Angel Island, but found no clues. The only evidence surfaced about four days later, when a black plastic waterproof bag containing photos belonging to Clarence Anglin was found floating in the water near Angel Island. The authorities believed this was proof that the escaped inmates had drowned. Those who believed the convicts had escaped argued that if they had drowned, at least one body would have been found floating on the water's surface. No one knows what really happened to Frank Lee Morris and Clarence and John Anglin.[17]

During Alcatraz's years as a federal prison, there were fourteen officially acknowledged escape attempts, involving a total of thirty-six men. Of these, one drowned, twenty-one were captured and returned, seven were killed by gunfire, two were recaptured and executed, and five are still missing. It is assumed that

Roe and Cole in 1937 and Morris and the Anglin brothers in 1962 also died.[18]

Alcatraz's reputation as an escape-proof prison was somewhat tarnished by the 1962 escape attempt, and the failure to account for the missing prisoners. The escape played a role in the changes that were coming to the island.

9

CONTROVERSY BRINGS CHANGE

Change was not new at Alcatraz. In 1948 Warden James Johnston retired. He was succeeded as warden by Edwin Swope and later Paul Madigan. As time passed, the harsh rules at the prison became somewhat more relaxed. Throughout the United States, the study of psychology led to new ways of treating prisoners. Some psychologists and authorities on crime and punishment believed that many criminals broke laws because they suffered from psychological problems caused by mental illness or from having been abused as children. Harsh punishment was considered inhumane and not particularly effective in changing a prisoner's behavior. Reforms such as therapy groups where inmates could talk about their problems with psychologists and in group sessions became popular at some prisons.

Over the years, the attitude of many prison officials at Alcatraz was that the prisoners there needed harsher treatment than those at other prisons. Warden Edwin

Swope said, "There is always a small minority needing an Alcatraz." Warden Paul Madigan said, "The men who come here have less prospect for rehabilitation than the men in the rest of our prison system."[1] Still, some changes were introduced to help inmates deal with the monotony of life at Alcatraz.

In the early 1950s, federal prison authorities in Washington, D.C., ordered Warden Swope to install a radio system. A loudspeaker system was installed among the plumbing pipes in the passageways between cells. To hear it, an inmate had to crouch down next to the vent opening by the toilet. Eventually, the system improved. Each inmate was given a set of earplugs. Cells were equipped with a jack so that inmates could listen to the radio from 6:00 P.M. to 9:30 P.M. Extra time was given on weekends and holidays. Prisoners did not have a wide choice of programs.[2]

Even with these improvements, Alcatraz continued to inspire criticism. Some critics complained that the cruel treatment, the monotony, and the isolation were uncivilized. Others complained of the secrecy under which Alcatraz was managed. Ernest Besig, director of the American Civil Liberties Union (ACLU) of northern California in the 1950s said: "When government officials operate in secrecy—when they do not have to account for their actions—they become immune to criticism. This is an invitation to mismanagement."[3]

Henry Elmer Barnes and Negley K. Teeters, prominent prison authorities of the 1950s, criticized Alcatraz's officials for having a basic philosophy that was unsound. The philosophy, they said, was that some prisoners cannot be reformed or changed and that the only way to handle them was with strict authority.[4]

Another criticism was that the prison was too expensive to run. In the late 1950s, keeping inmates at Alcatraz cost the government more than twice as much as at other federal prisons. Food costs were higher because everything, including water, had to be brought by boat to the island. In 1953 United States Senator William Langer told the Senate that it would be cheaper for the government to send the inmates to the Waldorf-Astoria, one of the most expensive hotels in New York City, than to keep them at Alcatraz. He added that it cost around $5 million a year to run the prison. At that time, there were only 150 inmates, which meant that each one cost the government $33,333.33 a year.[5] In addition, very little money was spent to rehabilitate the inmates. Other prisons had much larger programs for training inmates to reenter society. By 1960, rehabilitation of prisoners had become popular with the public and with prison officials. This concept stressed attempting to change prisoners' behavior through therapy and educational programs rather than through stern punishment.[6]

At Alcatraz, some of the strict rules were relaxed. When Olin Blackwell became warden in 1961, he allowed the inmates to buy a greater variety of things with the money they earned. Some of the inmates used their money to buy needles and yarn. Inmates could be seen knitting and crocheting in their cells. While they could not keep the items for their own use, they could send handmade bedspreads, babies' booties, and sweaters out of the prison as gifts.[7]

In 1961 closing the prison was discussed when it was determined that badly needed repairs would cost at least $5 million. The concrete cell walls were breaking down, making the prison insecure. Attorney General Robert Kennedy announced that a new federal maximum-security prison would be built at Marion, Illinois. Rumors circulated that the new prison would replace Alcatraz.[8]

The Morris–Anglin escape attempt on June 11, 1962, also pointed out that the prison was not as secure as had been thought. The inmates had been able to tunnel through the walls in a few weeks by using spoons. In response to the escape, the Bureau of Prisons suspended two officers for thirty days without pay. The officers had passed the lifelike dummies the inmates had placed in their cells without noticing that anything was wrong. The associate warden was transferred to a minimum-security prison, an unofficial way to show that the Bureau of Prisons was displeased with his performance on the job.[9]

Then, in December 1962, six months after the daring escape, two more inmates got out. John Paul Scott, a bank robber serving a thirty-year term, and Darl Lee Parker, a bank robber serving a fifty-year term, loosened the bars over a storeroom window in the kitchen area by using a saw made from strings soaked in wax and covered with cleanser to cut through the steel. They squeezed through the small window and climbed up a pipe to the roof. Using an electrical cord they had stolen as a rope, they escaped to the ground.

They placed inflated rubber surgical gloves in their pants to help them float. The men then jumped into the cold water. Parker was only able to get about fifty feet from the island before he became too weak to go farther. Scott was able to get as far as Fort Point, at the southern end of the Golden Gate Bridge. Several teenagers saw him and called the police. He was taken to the hospital and later returned to Alcatraz.[10]

Newspaper reports about the escape attempt brought more bad publicity to the prison. On March 21, 1963, Attorney General Kennedy officially closed Alcatraz Federal Penitentiary. The principal reasons given were the high expense of repairing and running the prison and the general feeling that inmates should be rehabilitated rather than isolated.[11]

The twenty-seven remaining prisoners were taken from the island, leaving 335 empty cells.[12] The island was turned over to the General Services Administration, the federal agency in charge of disposing of surplus government property. John Hart, a former guard, and his wife, Marie, stayed on the island as caretakers.[13]

Alcatraz and the American Indians

Closing Alcatraz Federal Penitentiary left the government with the problem of what to do with the rusting and deteriorating prison. It cost twenty-four thousand dollars a year to maintain the island until a new use could be found. Various suggestions were considered. They included turning the prison into a gambling casino, a wax museum, or an art museum. A presidential commission recommended building a monument on the island to honor San Francisco as the birthplace of the United Nations in 1945.

Some American Indians had ideas of their own. On March 8, 1964, a group of five men from the Sioux tribe occupied the island for several hours. They filed a claim for the island based on an 1864 treaty giving their tribe the right to claim unused federal property. They offered the government $5.64, or 47 cents an acre, for Alcatraz. This was the amount that the federal government had offered to pay the California tribes for

The last twenty-seven inmates left Alcatraz on March 21, 1963, and were transferred to other prisons. Alcatraz Federal Penitentiary then closed.

land taken by whites after the gold rush. When the General Services Administration ignored their claim, the Sioux went away.[14]

In the following months, more ideas for using the island were considered. The city of San Francisco wanted to use it for a park. The public was also asked for ideas. Some wanted to keep the prison buildings. Others said to tear them down. Millionaire Lamar Hunt suggested turning the prison into a village with an 1890s theme. Hunt also wanted to build a 364-foot space tower. William T. Workman, a descendant of Julian Workman, the man who had owned the island in the 1840s, made a claim for the island to be returned to his family.

On November 20, 1969, a larger group of American Indians landed on Alcatraz. Although their exact number is not known, it is estimated that the group numbered between eighty and one hundred. Most were students. They called themselves "Indians of All Tribes," and their spokesman was Richard Oakes. Oakes presented the General Services Administration officials with a list of demands. The group wanted to use the island for American Indian studies, a spiritual center, an ecology center, a training school, and a museum.

Their demands were based on their desire to make up for the injustices that the United States government

On November 20, 1969, a group of American Indians landed on Alcatraz and began an occupation of the island.

had inflicted for years on American Indians. They were also concerned that Alcatraz would become a tourist trap. Their occupation of the island focused national attention on the plight of American Indians. During their year-and-a-half stay on the island, the protesters organized an Alcatraz police force, whose members wore jackets that were hand-painted with the words "Alcatraz Security" and decorated with a tepee design. Stella Leach, a licensed vocational nurse, set up a medical clinic in the cell that had been occupied by Robert Stroud, the Birdman of Alcatraz.[15]

At first, there was some public support for the American Indian occupation because people were sensitive to the Indians' loss of lands and to the prejudice they sometimes suffered. In the city of Oakland, the Hell's Angels motorcycle gang held a party in support of the Indians' cause. An African-American group, the Black Panthers, offered medicine and blankets. The Jewish Woman's Organization donated twenty-five hundred dollars. Electrical generators were donated by the United Auto Workers union and the First United Church of San Francisco. At Thanksgiving, restaurant owners sent turkeys. John Trudell, a student from Los Angeles, began a radio program called "Radio Free Alcatraz," where he argued for the American Indians' cause.[16]

Arguments broke out between conflicting groups of American Indians over who would control the island. One group, the Thunderbirds, came armed with chains and pipes that they used to beat up others living on the island. There were also problems with alcohol and drug abuse.

Negotiations between the government and the American Indians continued. In a printed proclamation, the Indians offered to buy Alcatraz Island for twenty-four dollars in glass beads and red cloth, a price similar to that paid to American Indians for Manhattan Island by Dutch colonists in the seventeenth century. They also

These masks were made by students who visited Alcatraz. They show how the students felt about the treatment of American Indians in the United States.

said they would develop several institutions on the island to promote American Indian culture and values. They had a great deal of public support, including that of actors Jane Fonda and Anthony Quinn.[17]

The federal government responded by saying that no negotiations would take place until the American Indians left the island. There seemed to be a standoff.

In January 1970, the youngest daughter of leader Richard Oakes fell from one of the buildings on Alcatraz and was killed. Oakes left soon afterward. A few months later, negotiations ended. The government had decided that Alcatraz would become a park. It offered to have an American Indian cultural center, but refused to build a university there. The American Indians replied that this was unacceptable. Slowly, many of the American Indians began to leave the island. On June 1, 1970, a number of fires broke out, destroying a number of the historic buildings and gutting the lighthouse. On June 11, 1971, twenty armed federal marshals removed the fifteen remaining American Indians from the island. The removal was nonviolent.

The occupation did make Americans more aware of the problems of American Indians and served as a symbol of their dreams for more respect. Every year, many American Indians still visit the island to honor their traditions.[18]

Golden Gate National Recreation Area

On February 2, 1973, a headline in the *San Francisco Chronicle* announced that "Alcatraz may open to the Public." A new national recreation area around San Francisco Bay had been created by Congress a few months earlier. The thirty-four thousand acres that made up the Golden Gate National Recreation Area included the twelve-acre Alcatraz Island. In October 1973, Alcatraz opened to visitors. It is the only former federal prison open to the public. Thirty American

Indians were among the first to visit the island. They proclaimed a victory. "If the Indians hadn't taken over this place it would now be a part of Lamar Hunt's space museum," said Adam Nordwall, their leader.[19]

Today, close to a million visitors board the tour boats that leave from San Francisco's Pier 41 to visit Alcatraz each year. Most do not know about the island's history as a fort and a military prison. They come because they are fascinated by the island's history as a harsh federal prison from which escape was almost impossible. Sometimes, a former prisoner or guard is on hand to answer questions.

Alcatraz Island remains one of California's most popular tourist attractions.

The National Park Service interprets all aspects of Alcatraz's development over the years to help people understand its history. Park rangers also point out the natural history that makes Alcatraz special. Visitors see flocks of birds that have returned to the island. Many birds just visit the island; others breed and make their nests there. The island is a refuge for the birds that feed in San Francisco Bay.

Through the years, Alcatraz has served as a beacon for ships passing through the Golden Gate and as a fort to protect United States interests as the country expanded to the Pacific. It has been an example of harsh justice. It has also been a symbol of the dreams of American Indians. As visitors walk through the now empty cell blocks, they think about what it might have been like to have been a prisoner there. They can step into a cell in the "hole" and wonder how an inmate could have endured weeks or months of darkness and despair in such a tiny space. They can look into the cells where the Anglin brothers and Frank Lee Morris planned their daring 1962 escape. Just as the inmates did, they can look through barred windows at the tall buildings of San Francisco, a short distance across the bay, a view that tempted inmates to plot to escape. Visitors leave Alcatraz with a deep sense of the island's isolation and an awareness of the sinister history of the most famous prison in the United States.

★ TIMELINE ★

1542—Explorer Juan Rodriguez Cabrillo sails along the coast of California, and claims Alta (Upper) California for the king of Spain.

1769—Sergeant Jose Ortega discovers San Francisco Bay.

1775—Spanish explorers Juan Manuel de Ayala and Jose Canizares chart the islands in the bay; Ayala names one island "Alcatraces" after the large number of pelicans seen there.

1822—Mexico gains independence from Spain and claims California as Mexican territory.

1846—*June 8*: Julian Workman obtains a land grant for Alcatraz Island and is ordered by the Mexican governor of California, Pío Pico, to build a lighthouse there.

The United States wins the Mexican-American War; California becomes a territory of the United States.

1850—California becomes a state.

1854—*June 1*: A forty-foot-tall lighthouse is put into operation on the island.

1859—*December*: Company H of the Third Artillery occupies Alcatraz, beginning a seventy-seven-year occupation of the island by the United States Army.

1898—*April 24*: Spain declares war against the United States over Cuban independence; During the war, soldiers guilty of military offenses are imprisoned on Alcatraz.

1906—*April 18*: After the San Francisco earthquake, prisoners from the San Francisco jail are taken to Alcatraz.

1909—A new lighthouse, still in operation, is built on the island; Alcatraz is named the United States Military Prison, Pacific Branch, Alcatraz Island.

1915—The army prison is renamed Pacific Branch, United States Disciplinary Barracks.

1933—The army announces that the military prison on Alcatraz Island would be closed; The federal government announces plans to make Alcatraz a federal prison for the most dangerous inmates in the federal prison system.

1934—*August 22*: The first trainload of inmates arrives at Alcatraz.

September 3: Another trainload of dangerous criminals arrives at the prison.

1936—*January 22*: A disturbance breaks out as prisoners go on a three-day strike to protest strict rules.

1937—*September*: Inmates go on an unsuccessful five-day strike to try to get radios and newspapers.

1938—*May 23*: A guard, Royal C. Cline, is killed when three inmates—Thomas Limerick, Rufus Franklin, and James Lucas—attempt to escape.

1946—*May 2*: An escape attempt by Bernard Coy, Marvin Hubbard, Sam Shockley, Joseph Cretzer, Miran Thompson, and Clarence Carnes leads to a riot that lasts until May 4; Two guards and three of the escapees are killed.

1962—*June 11*: Frank Lee Morris and John and Clarence Anglin attempt to escape through air vents at the back of their cells; Their fate is still unknown.

1963—*March 21*: Attorney General Robert Kennedy orders Alcatraz federal prison closed; The last inmates leave.

1964—*March 8*: Five members of the Sioux tribe land on Alcatraz and occupy the island for several hours.

1969—*November 20*: A group of eighty to one hundred American Indians lands on Alcatraz; They call themselves "Indians of All Tribes;" They occupy the island until June 11, 1971.

1973—*October*: Alcatraz Island opens to the general public as part of the Golden Gate National Recreation Area.

★ Chapter Notes ★

Chapter 1. The Rock

1. Pierre Odier, *The Rock, A History of Alcatraz: The Fort/The Prison* (Eagle Rock, Calif.: L'Image Odier, 1982), pp. 110–111.

2. Frank J. Taylor, "Trouble Calls," *Colliers*, July 25, 1936, p. 10.

3. James P. Delgado, *Alcatraz: The Story Behind the Scenery* (Las Vegas: KC Publications, 1996), p. 27.

4. J. Campbell Bruce, *Escape from Alcatraz* (New York: McGraw-Hill Book Company, Inc., 1963), p. 26.

5. Odier, p. 129.

6. Delgado, pp. 31–33.

7. National Park Service, "Frequently Asked Questions Regarding Alcatraz's Federal Prison History, 1934–1963," *Alcatraz Island: Golden Gate National Recreation Area*, November 14, 1997, <http://www.nps.gov/alcatraz/>.

Chapter 2. Early Settlements

1. James P. Delgado, *Alcatraz: The Story Behind the Scenery* (Las Vegas: KC Publications, 1996), pp. 5–6.

2. Pierre Odier, *The Rock, A History of Alcatraz: The Fort/The Prison* (Eagle Rock, Calif.: L'Image Odier, 1982), pp. 18–23.

3. John A. Martini, *Fortress Alcatraz, Guardian of the Golden Gate* (Kailua, Hawaii: Pacific Monograph, 1990), pp. 9–11.

4. Odier, pp. 26–29.

5. Ibid., p. 29.

Chapter 3. Fort and Lighthouse

1. James P. Delgado, *Alcatraz: Island of Change* (San Francisco: Golden Gate National Parks Association, 1991), p. 10.

2. John A. Martini, *Fortress Alcatraz, Guardian of the Golden Gate* (Kailua, Hawaii: Pacific Monograph, 1990), pp. 19–27.

3. Pierre Odier, *The Rock, A History of Alcatraz: The Fort/The Prison* (Eagle Rock, Calif.: L'Image Odier, 1982), pp. 44–46.

4. Ibid., pp. 50–51.

5. Martini, pp. 36–37.

6. James P. Delgado, *Alcatraz: The Story Behind the Scenery* (Las Vegas: KC Publications, 1996), pp. 12–13.

7. Martini, p. 53.

8. Ibid., p. 51.

9. Ibid., p. 52.

10. National Park Service, "Fortress Alcatraz," *Alcatraz Island: Golden Gate National Recreation Area*, November 14, 1997, <http://www.nps.gov/alcatraz>.

Chapter 4. Alcatraz Military Prison

1. John A. Martini, *Fortress Alcatraz, Guardian of the Golden Gate* (Kailua, Hawaii: Pacific Monograph, 1990), pp. 61–66.

2. Ibid., pp. 81–82.

3. Ibid., pp. 68–71.

4. Pierre Odier, *The Rock, A History of Alcatraz: The Fort/The Prison* (Eagle Rock, Calif.: L'Image Odier, 1982), p. 78.

5. Martini, pp. 77–79.

6. Ibid., p. 78.

7. Odier, p. 79.

8. Martini, p. 80.

9. Ibid., p. 99.

10. Ibid., pp. 103–107, 156.

11. Odier, pp. 87–89.

12. Ibid., p. 88.

13. John Godwin, *Alcatraz, 1868–1963* (New York: Doubleday & Co., 1963), p. 32.

14. Martini, pp. 117–119.

Chapter 5. Federal Prison

1. James P. Delgado, *Alcatraz: The Story Behind the Scenery* (Las Vegas: KC Publications, 1996), p. 21.

2. "Prohibition," *Compton's Interactive Encyclopedia, Edition 1995*, 1992–1996, SoftKey Multimedia, Inc.

3. John Godwin, *Alcatraz, 1868–1963* (New York: Doubleday & Co., 1963), p. 34.

4. John Bartlow Martin, *Break Down the Walls: American Prisons, Past Present and Future* (New York: Ballantine Books, 1954), p. 146.

5. Godwin, pp. 34–36.

6. Pierre Odier, *The Rock, A History of Alcatraz: The Fort/The Prison* (Eagle Rock, Calif.: L'Image Odier, 1982), p. 98.

7. James A. Johnston, *Alcatraz Island Prison and the Men Who Live There* (New York: Charles Scribner's Sons, 1949), p. 13.

8. Ibid.

9. Godwin, pp. 79–81.

10. Johnston, p. 131.

11. Ibid., pp. 81–82.

12. Delgado, p. 26.

13. Odier, p. 104.

14. Godwin, p. 82.

15. John Kobler, *Capone: The Life and World of Al Capone* (New York: G. P. Putnam Sons, 1971), pp. 355–359.

Chapter 6. Prison Life

1. James A. Johnston, *Alcatraz Island Prison and the Men Who Live There* (New York: Charles Scribner's Sons, 1949), p. 22.

2. Pierre Odier, *The Rock, A History of Alcatraz: The Fort/The Prison* (Eagle Rock, Calif.: L'Image Odier, 1982), p. 147.

3. Ibid., p. 116.

4. Ibid., pp. 113–115.

5. J. Campbell Bruce, *Escape from Alcatraz* (San Francisco: Comstock Editions, Inc., 1976), p. 44.

6. Ibid., p. 39.

7. Odier, p. 116.

8. John Kobler, *Capone: The Life and World of Al Capone* (New York: G. P. Putnam Sons, 1971), p. 360.

9. Bruce, pp. 45–47.

10. Odier, p. 116.

11. James P. Delgado, *Alcatraz: The Story Behind the Scenery* (Las Vegas: KC Publications, 1996), p. 31.

12. Odier, pp. 143–144.

13. John Godwin, *Alcatraz, 1868–1963* (New York: Doubleday & Co., 1963), p. 81.

14. Odier, p. 141.

15. Bruce, pp. 79–92.

16. Odier, pp. 118–142.

17. James P. Delgado, *Alcatraz: Island of Change* (San Francisco: Golden Gate National Parks Association, 1991), pp. 34–35.

18. Jolene Babyak, *Eyewitness on Alcatraz* (Berkeley: Ariel Vamp Press, 1988), pp. 10, 16.

19. Ibid., p. 17.

20. Ibid., pp. 20, 45–49.

21. Ibid., pp. 56–57.

22. Ibid., pp. 61–63.

23. Delgado, *Alcatraz: Island of Change*, pp. 35–36.

Chapter 7. The Prisoners of Alcatraz

1. James A. Johnston, *Alcatraz Island Prison and the Men Who Live There* (New York: Charles Scribner's Sons, 1949), pp. 29–31.

2. John Kobler, *Capone: The Life and World of Al Capone* (New York: G. P. Putnam Sons, 1971), pp. 365–373.

3. Alvin Karpis and Robert Livesey, *On the Rock, Twenty-five Years in Alcatraz* (New York: Beaufort Books, Inc., 1980), foreword.

4. Pierre Odier, *The Rock, A History of Alcatraz: The Fort/The Prison* (Eagle Rock, Calif.: L'Image Odier, 1982), p. 220.

5. John Godwin, *Alcatraz, 1868–1963* (New York: Doubleday & Co., 1963), pp. 95–99.

6. Odier, p. 215.

7. Ibid., pp. 211–212.

8. Thomas E. Gaddis, *Birdman of Alcatraz* (Mattituck, N.Y.: Aeonian Press, 1976), pp. 179–181.

9. Ibid., pp. 182, 197.

10. Odier, pp. 212–213.

11. J. Campbell Bruce, *Escape from Alcatraz* (New York: McGraw-Hill Book Company, Inc., 1963), pp. 225–226.

12. Charles Jellison, "The Prisoner and the Professor," *Stanford Magazine*, March/April 1997, pp. 65–71.

13. Ibid., p. 71.

Chapter 8. Escapes and Riots

1. J. Campbell Bruce, *Escape from Alcatraz* (San Francisco: Comstock Editions, Inc., 1976), pp. 50, 51.

2. Ibid., p. 53.

3. Jolene Babyak, *Eyewitness on Alcatraz* (Berkeley: Ariel Vamp Press, 1988), pp. 34, 42.

4. James Fuller, *Alcatraz Federal Penitentiary, 1834–1963* (San Francisco: Asteron Productions, 1997), pp. 24–26.

5. Bruce, pp. 56–58.

6. Ibid., p. 61.

7. Ibid., pp. 62–63.

8. Ibid., pp. 70–74.

9. Fuller, p. 28.

10. Bruce, pp. 101–105.

11. Pierre Odier, *The Rock, A History of Alcatraz: The Fort/The Prison* (Eagle Rock, Calif.: L'Image Odier, 1982), p. 193.

12. James P. Delgado, *Alcatraz: The Story Behind the Scenery* (Las Vegas: KC Publications, 1996), p. 34.

13. Odier, p. 217.

14. Fuller, pp. 38–39.

15. Delgado, p. 35.

16. Ibid., pp. 40–41.

17. Bruce, pp. 193–194.

18. Babyak, p. 70.

Chapter 9. Controversy Brings Change

1. J. Campbell Bruce, *Escape from Alcatraz* (San Francisco: Comstock Editions, Inc., 1976), p. 195.

2. Pierre Odier, *The Rock, A History of Alcatraz: The Fort/The Prison* (Eagle Rock, Calif.: L'Image Odier, 1982), p. 132.

3. Bruce, p. 209.

4. Ibid., p. 208.

5. Ibid., p. 207.

6. Odier, p. 222.

7. Ibid., p. 206.

8. Ibid., p. 222.

9. Jolene Babyak, *Eyewitness on Alcatraz* (Berkeley: Ariel Vamp Press, 1988), pp. 119–120.

10. James Fuller, *Alcatraz Federal Penitentiary, 1834–1963* (San Francisco: Asteron Productions, 1997), p. 41.

11. Odier, p. 222.

12. James P. Delgado, *Alcatraz: Island of Change* (San Francisco: Golden Gate National Parks Association, 1991), p. 36.

13. Bruce, p. 215.

14. Ibid.

15. Odier, pp. 226–231.

16. Ibid., pp. 231–233.

17. Ibid., pp. 233–237.

18. Delgado, pp. 43–44.

19. Odier, p. 239.

★ FURTHER READING ★

Books

Altman, Linda Jacobs. *The California Gold Rush in American History*. Springfield, N.J.: Enslow Publishers, Inc., 1997.

Babyak, Jolene. *Eyewitness on Alcatraz*. Berkeley: Ariel Vamp Press, 1988.

Bruce, J. Campbell. *Escape from Alcatraz*. New York: McGraw-Hill Book Company, Inc., 1963.

Delgado, James P. *Alcatraz: Island of Change*. San Francisco: Golden Gate National Parks Association, 1991.

———. *Alcatraz: The Story Behind the Scenery*. Las Vegas: KC Publications, 1996.

Fuller, James. *Alcatraz Federal Penitentiary, 1934–1963*. San Francisco: Asteron Productions, 1997.

Heaney, Frank, and Guy Machado. *Inside the Walls of Alcatraz*. Palo Alto, Calif.: Bull Publishing Company, 1987.

Martini, John A. *Fortress Alcatraz, Guardian of the Golden Gate*. Kailua, Hawaii: Pacific Monograph, 1990.

Odier, Pierre. *The Rock, A History of Alcatraz: The Fort/The Prison*. Eagle Rock, Calif.: L'Image Odier, 1982.

Internet

Johnson, Troy. *The American Indian Occupation of Alcatraz Island, 1969–1971*. September 29, 1995. <http://www.acs.csulb.edu/~aisstudy/alcatraz/> (March 4, 1998).

National Park Service. *Alcatraz Island: Golden Gate National Recreation Area*. November 14, 1997. <http://www.nps.gov/alcatraz/> (March 4, 1998).

★ INDEX ★